UNDERSTANDING AND TREATING DISSOCIATIVE IDENTITY DISORDER (OR MULTIPLE PERSONALITY DISORDER)

UNDERSTANDING AND TREATING DISSOCIATIVE IDENTITY DISORDER (OR MULTIPLE PERSONALITY DISORDER)

Jo L. Ringrose

Routledge
Taylor & Francis Group

LONDON AND NEW YORK

First published 2012 by Karnac Books Ltd.

Published 2018 by Routledge
2 Park Square, Milton Park, Abingdon, Oxon OX14 4RN
711 Third Avenue, New York, NY 10017, USA

Routledge is an imprint of the Taylor & Francis Group, an informa business

British Library Cataloguing in Publication Data

A C.I.P. for this book is available from the British Library

ISBN-13: 9781780490335 (pbk)

Typeset by V Publishing Solutions Pvt Ltd., Chennai, India

For Mark, Laura, and Chris

CONTENTS

ACKNOWLEDGEMENTS

I would like to thank my clients for sharing all their experiences so bravely with me. They think I teach them but the learning and experience has come from them more than me.

Many, many thanks too to Dr Claire Schulz who has made substantial contributions to my clinical practice and greatly influenced my thinking and approach to working with these clients.

Similarly, I am also indebted to Dr Barbara Boat, Dr Erica Pearl, and all my research participants who gave up their free time to talk to me about their experiences in this field. I am grateful to you all; without your knowledge and experience the research and this book would be much the poorer.

I also want to thank Dr Ellert Nijenhuis and his colleagues at the Top Referent Centre in the Netherlands, some of whom subsequently kindly debated and critiqued elements of my research.

Special appreciation too to Dr Frank Putnam and Dr Carlson who have given permission for me to include the dissociative experiences scale, and to Dr Nijenhuis, Professor Spinhoven, Dr Van Dyck, Professor Van Der Hart and Dr Vanderlinden for their permission to include the SDQ-20. Also thanks for their substantial writings in this field that have helped me enormously, particularly initially when I needed people to shed light on what felt like a very bewildering disorder when I encountered my first client.

Thank you too to Remy Aquarone who was my academic consultant throughout my research. Remy has kindly agreed to me including here his method of assessment that can be used to score the level of functioning in clients with Dissociative Identity Disorder. Remy you helped me professionally but also personally to rise to the challenges of this work in my writing and practice; your support, particularly in those beginning days, was invaluable.

I am grateful too to Dr Colin Feltham for editing and proofreading the manuscript and to colleagues at the Metanoia Institute, in particular, Maxine Daniels and Val Thomas, who have been companions on my research journey and have provided both emotional and practical support, as well as critical ears to check out my ideas.

I also want to express my appreciation for fellow researchers and writers in this field, in particular, Dr Rick Kluft, Dr Richard Loewenstein, Dr Colin Ross, and Dr Mary Steinberg, whose written works have informed my understanding and shaped my therapy practice with this client group.

Lastly, love, thanks, and gratitude to my husband, Mark, for all the proofreading and computer support, and to my two children, Laura and Christopher, for their design ideas for the front and back covers, and my dear friend Julia Nadal, who along with my family has patiently listened to my accounts of the trials and tribulations throughout and fed me love, care, and enthusiasm when my resources have depleted.

ABOUT THE AUTHOR

Jo Ringrose BSc MA DPsych (Prof.) is a UKCP registered psychotherapist, a hypnotherapist and is director of The Karuna Centre for psychotherapy and Counselling, Harrogate, UK. She won an award for her research at Leeds University in 2001, has published articles, and regularly runs seminars and workshops in the field of trauma and dissociation.

PREFACE

My research for a doctorate in psychotherapy at the Metanoia Institute, London, involved me interviewing eight practitioners who specialise in the field of complex trauma and dissociation and who work on a regular basis with clients with Dissociative Identity Disorder (DID), or Dissociative Disorder Not Otherwise Specified (DDNOS). In the interviews, I asked these specialists open-ended questions about their work with this client group. The majority of the participants were working in specialist centres for the treatment of trauma and dissociation and were therefore immersed in this field of work and had considerable experience. They were sourced by searching the Internet for the names of some of the most widely known specialists in the field. The participants came from America, the Netherlands, and the UK. The questions I asked looked at all aspects of working with this client group, from the initial assessment, through their entire treatment, and included asking about some of the problems that these practitioners face in this work. The input from these specialists has been invaluable to me, and not wanting the material to simply sit on an academic shelf, I decided to incorporate it into a series of books. This book aims to be accessible to anyone who is just beginning working with someone they suspect may have DID (also known as Multiple Personality Disorder) or DDNOS. The material has also been derived from a search of the work published on the subject over the last thirty years, as well as being informed by my own experience of working with this client group. I hope you find it informative and would very much like to hear your comments. You can contact me, via the email address Jo@karunatherapy.co.uk.

CHAPTER ONE

The dissociative disorders and the presentation of Dissociative Identity Disorder (DID), or Multiple Personality Disorder (MPD)

The background of clients with Dissociative Identity Disorder

The vignettes I outline in this book have been based on an amalgamation of several clients' experiences. They aim to depict the two main underlying issues, that of attachment problems and repeated trauma, which clients with DID have experienced. Any likeness to someone's true life story is purely coincidental.

Vignette

Kerry is twenty-eight years old and currently lives alone. She lived with her mother and stepfather until she was fourteen when she ran away from home to escape sexual abuse by her stepfather and her uncle. In addition, her mother is an alcoholic and often got angry and violent with Kerry when drunk. The sexual abuse and violence had gone on for as long as Kerry can remember. Her biological father left the marital home when Kerry was two and had been out of contact since. Kerry had never got on well with her mother but the relationship broke down completely after she had told her about her stepfather's abuse and her mum had not believed her.

1

At school, teachers reported that Kerry seemed a very bright and able pupil who had achieved some high grades on occasion but lacked concentration and consistently good results. She was also branded a troublemaker after apparently being the ringleader in a binge-drinking episode in the school. At twelve, she was found passed out in the school toilets, after she had cut both wrists having been raped by her stepfather the previous day. She was seen by a psychiatrist who asked about her family but she felt unable to tell anyone. She returned home after treatment having nowhere else to go and went back to school but from the age of thirteen missed more days than she attended.

Kerry left home at fourteen, slept rough, and prostituted herself in order to buy alcohol and food. She was picked up by social services who found her a place of safety with foster parents but unfortunately the foster father became ill and she had to be moved to a further home six months later. The relationship she had with the second foster parents had a bad start with Kerry's drinking increasing at this time. After several months, they said they could not cope with her. At this point she was fifteen and decided she wanted to live alone. She was moved to temporary sheltered housing until she was considered able to live independently.

Currently Kerry is not working. She would like to go to college but states that there is too much getting in the way. She reports losing time and having no memory of what has gone on during these blank spells. She says she finds herself coming-to in strange places, not knowing how she got there, or why she is there. This frightens her because she was found wandering the streets in her nightdress one night at three in the morning and had to be taken home by the police. Her arms are filled with scars from cutting but she says that she does not cut herself. She states that she comes-to afterwards and it is like someone else has done it. When I ask if she has ever found anything that she does not recognise in her belongings she pulls out a small book with handwriting and pictures. She says that she does not know the artist or the one with the frilly handwriting. Neither, she says, are hers.

This is the typical background of someone with DID. These clients tend to have both attachment issues and repeated trauma, which is almost without exception sexual abuse; many are neglected in addition. The necessity of a good therapy relationship is paramount in all therapy work. However, with this client group, this point cannot be over emphasised. It is from this therapy relationship and the development of a safe base that the client learns she is valuable, worthy of love and care, and that relationships can be supportive. A strong therapy relationship challenges the client's belief system that she is in some way deficient or not worthy of love, and this new knowledge and experience can be carried into further relationships outside of therapy. In addition, it is from this secure safe base that therapy can begin the process of fostering communication, collaboration, and co-operation between the identities and, where necessary, the trauma incidents can be worked through.

Definition of dissociation and the dissociative disorders

"The essential feature of the dissociative disorders is a disruption in the usually integrated functions of consciousness, memory, identity and perception" (American Psychiatric Association, 2000, p. 519).

The five dissociative disorders, as outlined by the American Psychiatric Association (2000) are Dissociative Amnesia (DA), Dissociative Fugue (DF), Depersonalization Disorder (DP), Dissociative Disorder Not Otherwise Specified (DDNOS), and Dissociative Identity Disorder (DID) (American Psychiatric Association, 2000; listed as "Multiple Personality Disorder" in the International Statistical Classification of Diseases and Related Problems, World Health Organization, 2007). This book contains information on working with DID and DDNOS—although, to avoid repetition, I have not written "and DDNOS" throughout the book. If you are a clinician working with a client with DDNOS the therapy that is advocated is sufficiently similar for it to apply.

Definition of Dissociative Identity Disorder

"Dissociative Identity Disorder (or Multiple Personality Disorder) is characterized by the presence of two or more distinct identities or personality states that recurrently take control of the individual's behaviour, accompanied by an inability to recall important personal information that is too extensive to be explained by ordinary forgetfulness. It is a disorder characterized by identity fragmentation, rather than proliferation of separate personalities" (American Psychiatric Association, 2000, p. 519).

Practitioners sometimes refer to clients with DID as having one or more host identities, one of whom tends to be the part who presented to therapy initially and one or more alter identities (see below). At present, treatment focuses on fostering communication and cooperation amongst the host(s) and alter(s), understanding and processing the trauma each identity has carried and sometimes, towards the end of therapy, there may be integration of the different identities.

Demographics of Dissociative Identity Disorder

Dissociative identity disorder has for many years been seen as a rare disorder and in ICD-10 is still classified as such. However, as awareness of the disorder and diagnostic instruments have improved, newer versions of DSM-IV have dropped the term rare in its descriptions. Steinberg (1994) wrote "in the past ten years studies have estimated the prevalence of DID to range from 1% and 10% in the psychiatric community".

Rifkin et al. (1998) found that one per cent of randomly selected women aged between 16 and 50 years old, who had recently been admitted to an acute psychiatric hospital, were found to have DID using the Structured Clinical Interview for DSM-IV Dissociative Disorders.

The vast majority of these are female. For example, a study of 50 consecutive patients with Dissociative Identity Disorder found that 88 per cent were female (Coon et al., 1988). The average age at diagnosis is between twenty-nine and thirty-five years (Allison, 1978 cited in Putnam, 1989; Coons et al., 1988).

The development of Dissociative Identity Disorder

A vignette

> At five years old Kerry was molested by her stepfather. During the molestation she got through it by imagining it was happening to someone else. Kerry imagined this sufficiently strongly for her to separate herself from the part of her that was abused, creating an alter personality—"someone else". The next time Kerry was abused by her stepfather "someone else" just came and took the abuse

which meant that Kerry could get on with her life. After a while Kerry forgot about "someone else" but when Kerry was alone with her stepfather she would become scared but did not know why, although "someone else" knew.

When Kerry was eleven, her uncle raped her. Kerry pretended it was happening to "anyone but her". Kerry saw "anyone but her" from the ceiling of her bedroom. Kerry believed "anyone but her" looked nothing like herself. Kerry left for a while and "anyone but her" took her place.

"Anyone but her" began drinking and smoking cannabis. "Anyone but her" was not like Kerry: Kerry let her curly hair run loose and liked pretty dresses; "anyone but her" wore her hair tied back, always wore jeans, and let no-one come close. Other people viewed "anyone but her" as a bully. "Anyone but her" knew about "someone else" and berated her for whingeing and getting upset. "Anyone but her" called "someone else" a baby and told her to shut up whenever "someone else" spoke.

At thirteen Kerry returned, causing "anyone but her" to retreat into the background for a while. Kerry was invited to a friend's party. She had to buy a dress, since all she could find in the wardrobe were jeans and T-shirts. Unbeknown to Kerry these had been chosen and worn by "anyone but her". Kerry put on her new dress, wore her hair loose, and said goodbye to her mother. Her mother said she had the old Kerry back. Kerry did not know what she meant. At the party, one minute Kerry was talking with friends; the next thing she remembered she was coming-to, slumped in her friend's hall with her friend's parents shouting at her. She could not understand it. She never got drunk. She did not even like drink. She said her drink must have been spiked, but her friend said she had left soon after arriving and returned with a bottle of vodka. Unbeknown to Kerry "anyone but her" had returned part way through the party, bought the drink, got drunk, and had now left, leaving Kerry to pick up the pieces.

On the way home, when Kerry was trying to explain things to her mother, "anyone but her" told Kerry to shut up, called her "a useless bag of shit", and told her that she would shut her up if she did not shut up of her own accord. Kerry went quiet.

Kerry began to lose time, with no memory of what happened for long spells during the day. On one occasion, Kerry found herself coming-to following an overdose of sleeping pills. Kerry had no memory at all of taking the pills. When Kerry's stepfather picked her up from the hospital he told her that she was a liar and of course she must know what had happened. Being called a liar and making excuses for behaviour she had no recollection of performing were becoming commonplace. Other strange things happened too. She had kept a diary for years and one day when she went to write in it, she found that it was full of a child's handwriting. Kerry did not know it but the handwriting belonged to "someone else".

The structure of the personality

The host

Frequently, initial contact in therapy is made by a host (sometimes referred to as the "Apparently Normal Personality" (ANP)) (Van der Hart et al., 2006: 5) as opposed to an alter identity. In the vignette, for simplicity's sake, the client had one host, Kerry. Where there is only one host, it is she who clients typically identify with as being "me". The host tends to be the part who has executive control of the body most of the time. However, often there are two or even several hosts (Van der Hart et al., 2006). As a general rule, the more identities there are, the longer that therapy will take, particularly if there are multiple hosts. Also, occasionally, the host may not be a single personality. Putnam (1989, p. 107) writes: "In some cases, the host is a social façade created by a more or less cooperative effort of several alters agreeing to pass as one." These alters may share the outside role and have similar but slightly different names.

The alter personalities

Kluft (1984) defines an alter personality (sometimes referred to as an Emotional Part (EP) (Van der Hart et al., 2006)) as:

> An entity with a firm, persistent and well-founded sense of self and a characteristic and consistent pattern of behaviour and feelings in response to given stimuli. It must have a range of functions, a range of emotional responses and a significant life history (of its own existence).

(Kluft, 1984, p. 23)

The alters view themselves as separate people and do not understand that they share the same body and that all of them together constitute a whole person. It is important that therapists do not go along with this belief and that they inform all identities that there is only one body and that harm by one identity harms all of the other identities, although as a therapist you can empathize with each identity's desire for separateness.

Child alters

In the vignette of Kerry above, "someone else" is one of Kerry's child alters. Child and infant alters are very common and are locked in the timeframe within which they were created. They often present as small, fragile-looking souls, frequently frightened, and need to be addressed in a manner appropriate to their age. These child alters are often crying out for attachment and pull on the heart strings of therapists, making it difficult for therapists to keep strict boundaries. Therapists can become drawn into mothering scared, sad, and lonely alters because they find it difficult to ignore their pleas. However, the host(s) and where appropriate, older alters, need to be encouraged to parent the child alters as much as possible, as it is this that will help them to grow up.

Persecutor and violent alters

As is often the case, Kerry also has an alter who persecutes the other identities: "anyone but her". In this instance, she wants to silence Kerry when she, or one of the other alters, tries to speak in therapy, or at other times. It is important for therapists to explain to all of the identities any consequences there may be if someone talks about their life story, particularly abuse or torture incidents, in therapy. Persecutor alters often function to silence the other identities because they fear bad consequences if a part talks about the perpetrators of trauma. Hence, they often want to kill off the host or another alter in order to silence them, but do not understand that this means that they will die too. Talking indirectly through the host, or where necessary, directly to the persecutory alter(s) early on in the process of meeting the alters, is vital. It can prevent suicide attempts and self-mutilation as these are less likely to occur once you have persecutory alters on board. Even if I do not know whether there is a persecutory alter or not, I will ask if anyone has any objections to anybody talking in therapy. If there are concerns, I will explore these and answer them as far as I can. This can also bring a sense of relief for therapist, host(s), and alter(s) alike. Occasionally it may be necessary to put a ban on talking about a particular event until all are satisfied with disclosure. In addition, it is important to find out from angry, aggressive, or persecutory alters what their rules are and to respect the boundaries of these alters. I explain that I do not wish to remove their authority but that I want to try to help them work through their problems (Ringrose, 2010).

Whilst I have never been confronted with a violent alter in private practice, bear in mind that they exist. I would advocate you take steps to manage the risks that these clients can pose. I choose not to work with clients from my own home, do not have my home telephone number listed in the telephone directory, and do not give details of my home address and home number to clients. One of my clients came to me after her previous therapist said she could no longer work with her. This was because the client would stand for hours outside her house. Also, some child alters are prone to texting and telephoning when they feel scared and if this were on your home telephone it could become a nuisance. More seriously, violent alters are capable of killing and may do so in response to child alters feeling vulnerable (Ringrose, 2010). Whilst working in forensic services, I worked with a woman who was incarcerated because of the actions of her scared persecutory alter. Also bear in mind, even if these alters are not physically hurting the host or other alters, they may control and persecute them, often leaving them frightened. Respect violent or persecutory alters and negotiate with them as much as possible. Find out what function they perform and why they were created. This is usually to protect the host. A goal for therapy is for all the identities to eventually get along; for example, explaining that the persecutory or violent alter(s) arose as a means of protecting them all, can help with this. Do all that you can to promote an ethos of pulling together in the fight against the aftermath of trauma and encourage all identities to be on the same side in this respect. Typically the host(s) or outside alter(s) just wish that the other identities would go away. This is even stronger where there are persecutory or violent alter(s). One of the most important tasks of the therapist is to encourage the identities to work together.

Helper alters

In addition to child and persecutor alters, there may be one or several helper alters. Initially these may present as helpless or as having little control or influence over what happens during therapy. However, as therapy gets underway they may be able to stave off violent attacks on the body (Putnam, 1989), or where attacks occur they may negotiate a switch and get help. Where there is no helper alter, one or more of the other alters can be encouraged to support the host when her energy levels are low and she is struggling to cope. There is often an identity who is super-efficient and hard-working, who can be encouraged to share the burden, thereby helping to occasionally maintain a level of stability when a host's resources are depleted.

There are further common types of alters, frequently one of the opposite sex to the host. For a more detailed look, Putnam (1989: Chapter Five) provides an excellent chapter outlining these.

Switching

Switching is the process of changing from one identity to another. Therefore a switch may occur from one alter to another alter, from a host to an alter, or an alter to a host. The most common times that switching occurs are when an identity is reminded of a past trauma event and the event acts as a trigger. Switching may also occur, however, in session when an alter wants to talk to the therapist. It is important to help the client work out what has triggered the switch because this often provides valuable information about the situations when switching is likely to occur and can be the beginning of gaining some control in this respect.

There are various clues suggesting that a client is switching in session. There may be facial changes, particularly changes in the position or gaze of the eyes, often accompanied by a single rapid movement of the head. Clients may be seen to blink rapidly or their gaze may be fixed with eyes slightly down to the left or right. Similarly there may be changes in their speech, for example, a different loudness, tone, accent, or vocabulary.

If I think clients have a lot to contain between sessions, I ask them to write about their troubles. This helps to prevent the identities becoming overwhelmed with material (Ringrose, 2010). The different alters may use different language, font sizes, colours, and styles; their handwriting often varies, and where clients draw pictures, these may be drawn in different styles or by using different drawing implements.

Further common signs of switching, or clues suggesting one or more identities are about in session, is when the host appears as though she is not listening, as if she is miles away, or she will not answer you when you ask a question and then apologise and say she did not hear you. Also, there may be rapid changes in her focus of attention to different trains of thoughts, or a pattern of saying something is so, often quite adamantly and then changing her mind. She may use "we" rather than "I", appear childlike and small at one time and confrontational and aggressive at another.

Switching can lead to confusion in the therapist as she can become unsure of who she is talking to, or whose interests are being worked on. These sorts of problems are common and impact on therapists and clients alike. One client said her experience of the other alters created such noise and confusion in her head that it felt like "popcorn going off in the microwave" (Ringrose, 2010).

As was the case with Kerry in the vignette, sometimes alters dress very differently, wearing their hair in a very different style where they may go from short dark hair, to getting hair extensions, or a colour, or perm. Similarly the alters' mannerisms, preferred posture and tastes vary. However, perhaps one of the most obvious changes is their rapid shifts in mood, which may be from depressed and anxious, to angry and hostile, in a short space of time.

* * *

Summary

- A host is typically one of the first identities to present in therapy. There may be one or more hosts. As a general rule, the more identities there are, the longer the client is likely to need in therapy.
- There will be one or more alters. The average is fifteen (Ross, 1997).
- Commonly there are child, persecutory, and helper alters.
- Switching is the process of changing from one identity to another.

CHAPTER TWO

Assessment and diagnosis

A stronger emphasis on assessment and diagnosis

Specialist practitioners working with clients with DID typically place considerable importance on screening, assessment, and diagnosis and will sometimes repeat tests throughout therapy to see how clients are progressing (Ringrose, 2010). Psychotherapy assessments are usually used to guide therapy. However, in the case of clients with DID, aside from facilitating the devising of a therapy plan, the work is likely to be long term and involve outside professionals. Therefore, in the UK, often diagnosis is used to make a plea for funding through the National Health Service (NHS), as well as being useful for liaising purposes. In this case, a detailed diagnosis is needed in order to make such a plea. Further to this, clients with DID pose a high risk of harm to themselves and sometimes other people, which practitioners want to feel competent they can work with.

Incorrect or missed diagnoses

However, the most important reason for a strong focus on assessment and diagnosis relates to practitioners' awareness of clients frequently receiving incorrect diagnoses. Kluft (1991) reported that the average length of time it takes for a client to receive a diagnosis of DID is just short of seven years. Nonetheless, diagnosis with these clients is vital because the client is multiple. Practitioners need to take all of the identities into account. Without this, clients are unlikely to significantly improve.

The high number of missed diagnoses are most likely to be due to practitioners' difficulty in identifying the disorder because it is often masked by other, often more obvious, conditions, such as anorexia. In addition, psychiatrists may misdiagnose because they have to find a drug treatment for their patient and since there are no known drug treatments for DID they may opt for the closest condition, typically schizophrenia, schizo-affective disorder, schizoid tendency, or bipolar disorder (Ringrose, 2010). There will also be clients who have a disso-ciative disorder that is co-morbid with another disorder, for example, borderline personality disorder, which adds to the confusion.

Due to my work with this client group, I have changed the questions I ask at the initial intake assessment. I believe that this is imperative for some practitioners given that there are differences which I feel are vitally important to consider right from the start of therapy with some-one with DID. Hence, I have always asked about previous self-harm and suicide incidents during the intake assessment but now I am more alert to the possibility of a client having DID where clients report high levels of self-harm and suicide attempts and where their histories con-tain all or most of the elements outlined below.

Features in the history of clients with Dissociative Identity Disorder

- A poor, insecure, or unpredictable attachment with a parent, parents, or parental figure.
- An emotionally or physically absent mother.
- Torture, neglect, physical, sexual, or emotional abuse, or repeated witnessing of domestic violence in the family home.
- Repeat admissions to accident and emergency (A&E) departments for self-harm or suicide attempts. Typically these occur within a short space of time, often twice in a weekend.
- Frequent or continuous contact with mental health services, com-monly since teenage years.
- A diagnosis of anxiety, depression, borderline personality disor-der, schizophrenia, schizo-affective disorder, manic depression, an

eating disorder, epilepsy, pseudo-seizures, or a history of addiction to alcohol or drugs.

Clients may or may not mention further symptoms, the most common of which I have summarised in the box "List of common symptoms".

However, certain symptoms may come to light as therapy progresses, such as trance states and signs of regression. Inconsistencies in the client's story may be one of the first signs that a client has DID. In such cases, the client appears as if she is lying. This is because the different identities often will have a different take on their memories, thoughts, feelings, and experiences, and the therapist may hear the accounts from each in turn. Sometimes this can result in members of the client's care team going to great lengths to ascertain the veracity of the client's story. This is not necessary and carries the potential to damage the client's relationship with one or more professionals. From a therapist's perspective, holding each of the identity's stories and their feelings, thoughts, and behaviours in relation to it is helpful.

List of common symptoms

- **Amnesia**—typically around trauma events but may be for large chunks of the client's childhood. There are also often amnesic barriers between the identities which effectively separate the alters' memories and experiences from the host and one another.
- **Anxiety**—which may appear to come out of nowhere and feel uncontainable.
- **Auditory hallucinations**—crying, muttering, self-deprecatory remarks, but where the clients know these come from inside their head.
- **Depression.**
- **Fugue episodes**—clients often find themselves at some known or unknown destination with no understanding of why they are there, or how they arrived.
- **Insomnia**—alters may keep the host and other alters awake. Often nightmares are reported too.
- **Lost time**—the host experiences lost time when the alter(s) take over the limelight for a while.
- **Low self-esteem.**

- **Mood swings**—too rapid to be bipolar disorder, as there may be several mood changes in a day.
- **Numbness**—or feeling distant, detached, or unreal, which often occurs just after a crisis.
- **Self-harm**—may be to try to prevent switching, to bring the client back from a distant/detached/unreal state, or to change an emotional pain into a physical one because this feels more controllable.
- **Somatoform symptoms**—see page 31.
- **Suicide attempts**—often in rapid succession and may be without the host's awareness.

If I suspect the client has DID but am still unsure, I will ask further questions. Clients may not answer yes to all of these questions in order for me to screen but they act as a strong indication of DID or DDNOS.

Key questions prior to full screening for DID

1. **Have you lost time? If so, how much and how often?**
   When clients lose time, this is indicative of them having another identity which they may, or may not, be aware of.
2. **Have you ever found yourself "come-to" somewhere but had no recollection of how you got there?**
   This question is asking about whether the client has fugue episodes.
3. **Have you ever heard voices in your head?**
   These are the voices of the other identities talking to one another and may be distinct, heard as mumbling, or completely absent. Clients may be reluctant to answer this question because they know that people with schizophrenia hear voices and therefore fear this diagnosis. However, this can be talked through with the client.
4. **Have you experienced physical symptoms where a known cause has never been established? (For example, difficulty swallowing, talking, or moving.)**
   Clients may present with physical symptoms without mentioning the more common problems found in DID. See below under Somatoform Dissociation Questionnaire (Nijenhuis et al., 1996).

Assessment of the client's functioning

Remy Aquarone (cited in Ringrose, 2010) outlined a checklist of eight items devised to assess the general level of functioning of clients with DID. With his permission, I have adapted these in order to fit them to a Likert scale that can be easily scored. These are outlined below. This can be used to give practitioners further indication of how long the client will be in therapy. The assessment can be undertaken at the initial assessment and can be used to reassess clients at further pertinent stages of treatment.

Using the scale of 1 to 4: where 1 = Excellent, 2 = Good, 3 = Fair, and 4 = Poor. Score the client's responses to the following questions:

1. How would you rate the host(s) level of communication, cooperation or co-presence among the identities? (How able is the host(s) to share day-to-day living?)
2. How would you rate the client's level of involvement in the community? (Is the client working or able to look after family, for example?)
3. How would you rate the strength of the host? (How much of the time is the host in executive control? Some clients are very controlled by young alters.)
4. How would you rate the client's social support system?

For the following questions use the same scoring from 1 to 4 but where 1 = Very low, 2 = Low, 3 = High, and 4 = Very High.

5. How would you rate the client's level of physical symptoms? (Where there are many physical complaints, change is slower and more problematic.)
6. What is the level of involvement of professionals in the client's care? (Someone who has numerous agencies involved is likely to need longer in therapy.)
7. What is the level of hospital admissions?
8. What is the level of psychotherapy input prior to current therapy? (Clients who have been in therapy for a protracted period of time before assessment are typically harder to treat.)

The client's score is derived by adding together the scores for each of the eight items. The total score is out of a maximum of thirty-two. Everything else being equal, the higher the score, the longer the client is likely to need in therapy.

Dissociative Experiences Scale (DES I and II)

Where I suspect that clients have DID, I follow this up by asking them to complete the Dissociative Experiences Scale (DES) (Carlson & Putnam, 1986). With the authors' permission a copy of the scale can be found in the resources section towards the back of this book. Also, at the time of writing, an electronic version, which scores responses for you, can be obtained online by visiting: http://counsellingresource.com/quizzes/des/index.html.

The scale is useful because the majority of clients with DID have the symptoms seen in the other dissociative disorders outlined in DSM-IV-TR: Dissociative Amnesia (DA), Dissociative Fugue (DF), and Depersonalisation (DP), as well as their behavioural manifestations, and the questions tap all of these. It is also useful to go through the DES with clients after they have completed it because this can help to validate their experiences. Clients may then begin to understand why they lose time, find strange things in their possession, or find themselves at a particular destination, and not know how they got there. This information can help to reduce their feeling of isolation too as they realize that they are not the only person with these problems. Lastly, it can help to increase clients' understanding of where their problems lie, highlighting what they may want to tackle in therapy (Ringrose, 2010).

The DES (Carlson & Putnam, 1986) comprises twenty-eight questions. It is important that the client completes the questions herself because it may be that one or more of the identities fill in part of it. A score over thirty is a strong indication of DID (Carlson et al., 1993).

The scale is the most widely used and studied instrument employed to screen for dissociative disorders (Simeon et al., 1998). The second version, the DES II (Carlson & Putnam, 1993; Ellason et al., 1991) is currently the most common form in use. However, the test is not intended to be used as a diagnostic tool for the assessment of DSM-IV dissociative disorders but rather as a screening instrument for the identification of clients with a dissociative disorder. The questions relate to a number of experiences that "some people" have and the client is required to circle a number to show what percentage of the time this happens to her. The test has been praised because it is easy to use and does not stigmatise the client. It has been criticised for having long-winded questions and for failing to examine the somatoform symptoms that clients with DID often face (Ringrose, 2010; Nijenhuis et al., 1996). The scale has been found to be internally consistent, reliable over time, and to have convergent and discriminant validity (Simeon et al., 1998; Carlson et al., 1993).

Example Statement from the DES II
"Some people have the experience of driving a car and suddenly realising that they don't remember what has happened during all or part of the trip. Circle a number to show what percentage of the time this happens to you."

The timing of the test is important because DID is an extremely hard diagnosis to digest. Hence, it is important to ensure that the client is ready and able to cope with this information. On realising that they have identities, clients report feeling like a "weirdo" and wanting to be "normal". By that they usually mean they do not want to know that they have these different identities, particularly if they are doing things that the host would not normally do. I help clients to manage these feelings by talking to them about the spectrum of dissociation. I explain that from time to time everyone will "log off" and report being miles away in their head and will not know what happened at those times. I also explain how we all have different sides to us. For example, I describe how sometimes I have a heart that says one thing and a head that says something else, or an inner child who wants to be playful when an adult self knows that we have to be sensible and work. I will also sometimes explain (depending on whether I think the client is ready or not) that whilst there are these similarities, perhaps the main difference between someone who has DID and someone who does not, is that the latter will typically be in executive control all of the time (except, for example, when the person is inebriated or concussed) whilst the former will not. I use this information to try to encourage the host to work with her identities, informing her that by getting to know them she can begin to stay in control for longer periods and reduce her lost time. I have found this the main motivating factor for doing this work, particularly at times when the host does not want to negotiate with a hostile alter, or one who is seen as a trouble maker.

Somatoform Dissociation Questionnaire (SDQ 20)

If I feel clients are ready, I will ask them to complete the twenty question version of the Somatoform Dissociation Questionnaire (SDQ-20, Nijenhuis et al., 1996; Nijenhuis et al., 1997). At the time of writing an electronic version can be resourced from www.psychotherapist.org/Sdq20 and scoring information is available at www.enijenhuis.nl/SDQ/sdq-update.doc. With the authors' permission I have included the test in the resources section at the back of this book. It is important to time this so that you feel that the client is sufficiently robust to cope with what the test confronts. Pacing of information is paramount so that the client does not start to feel overwhelmed. Clients with DID may report the somatoform symptoms found in the SDQ-20 more readily than, say, lapses in memory or lost time. This can be because for this group of patients, these experiences are more salient than some of those mentioned in the DES II, or it may be that the trauma is only experienced as a physical symptom(s).

The SDQ-20 comprises twenty statements. Clients are asked the extent to which the symptom or experience outlined in the statement applies to them and to rate their response using a Likert type scale from 1 to 5. In addition, clients are asked to circle yes or no to the question "Is the physical cause known?" and where known, for it to be named. Questions are clear and all begin with "It sometimes happens that." The test is easy to administer and clients tend to complete it in less than half an hour. Scoring involves a simple summation of scores from the Likert scale. The authors of the questionnaire recommend that therapists do not adjust the scores where clients report a known cause of a physical symptom. Nijenhuis et al. (2003) reported excellent internal consistency and construct validity. In addition, like the DES and other tests for dissociative disorders, clients with DID score significantly higher on this test, compared with clients with DDNOS. Example statements from the SDQ-20 are in the box below.

Example statements from the SDQ-20

"I have trouble urinating."
"I have an attack which resembles an epileptic seizure."
"I am paralysed for a while."

Somatoform dissociative symptoms are often very powerful memories associated with abusive pasts (Ross et al., 1989). For example, one of my clients reported feeling tightness around her ankles, which later we discovered related to her being tied up. However, symptoms may be described in more general terms where they do not relate to a specific trauma incident so directly. A further client has reported having a red ball made out of elastic bands rolling around in her stomach.

A practitioner who participated in my research mentioned one of her clients who described a constant arguing inside himself. At the beginning of therapy, he did not experience arguing in his head but in his body. He said he did not hear voices but felt them inside as if there was a constant knocking and pulling in different parts of his body (Ringrose, 2010). Further common complaints are physical symptoms due to the original fight, flight, freeze, or total submission response. Hence, clients may report pounding heart, sweaty palms, or feeling a desire to run.

Somatoform dissociative symptoms intrude on the host, making it hard for her to function and cope with daily tasks. Some practitioners use a phenomenological categorisation system where each somatoform symptom may be classified into positive or negative. Positive somatoform dissociative symptoms are intrusive symptoms which result in there being too much of something, for example, pain or body movements (e.g., tics). Negative somatoform dissociative symptoms are observed as a loss of an ability, for example, an inability to move or speak, which is typical of a freeze response (Ringrose, 2010). In the "List of common somatoform dissociative symptoms" below I list some of the most common somatoform symptoms.

List of common somatoform dissociative symptoms
• Any inexplicable pain • Heart problems • Difficulty swallowing • Paralysis or numbness in one or more body parts • Fainting • Speaking in a whisper / An inability to speak for short periods • Genital pain • Stomach ache

- Headaches
- Problems urinating
- Seizures which have no neurological basis
- Physical sensations related to the body's fight, flight and freeze response, e.g., pounding heart.

Structured Clinical Interview for DSM-IV Dissociative Disorders (SCID-D and SCID-D-R)

Where practitioners in the UK are seeking funding for their client's therapy, they are likely to need to use the Structured Clinical Interview for DSM-IV Dissociative Disorders (the SCID-D) in order to substantiate their claim. The SCID-D was the first diagnostic instrument developed for the assessment and diagnosis of a dissociative disorder (Steinberg, 1993). The revised version, SCID-D-R (Steinberg, 1994), emerged one year later. It is a semi-structured interview containing questions on psychiatric history and consisting of approximately 150 to 260 questions depending on the client's answers. There are both direct and indirect questions looking at symptoms from a subjective and behavioural perspective. In addition, the interviewer rates the client as to whether or not:

- A given symptom is present and at what severity (1: absent to 4: severe; the total score ranges from 5 to 20).
- The DMS-IV criteria for a dissociative disorder have been met.

Cues suggestive of a dissociative disorder such as spontaneous age regression, trance-like appearance, and amnesia are recorded, as are inconsistencies amongst the client's responses. Diagnosis is achieved through an assessment of the constellation of symptoms.

Evaluation of the SCID-D-R

The SCID-D-R has been translated into several languages. It has also been found to have good to excellent inter-rater reliability and discriminant validity for diagnosing the five dissociative disorders (Draijer & Boon, 1993). It is the most widely used diagnostic tool used to confirm a diagnosis of a dissociative disorder and is useful in terms of helping clients feel understood and for them to have their symptoms validated. In this respect it can help clients begin to face their disorder.

It is very thorough in most respects but has been criticised for not containing items looking for somatoform and conversion symptoms (Nijenhuis et al., 1997) and for not being very accessible (Cardeña & Weiner, 2004). The main drawbacks to using the SCID-D-R are that practitioners require training and supervision (Steinberg & Schnall, 2000); a knowledge of DSM-IV diagnostic criteria; a familiarity of the literature on dissociation; knowledge of the interviewer's guide; and the test takes from two to three hours to administer, which paying clients may not wish to pay for (Ringrose, 2010). For these reasons, private practitioners not pursuing funding are unlikely to use it.

Further available tests are the Dissociative Disorder Interview Schedule (DDIS) (Ross et al., 1989b) and the Office Mental State Examination for Complex Chronic Dissociative Symptoms and Multiple Personality Disorder (Loewenstein, 1991). I have found both of these useful in terms of helping me to understand the disorder and its symptoms.

* * *

Summary

Assessment and diagnosis is important because:

- Diagnoses are being missed. Where this occurs, the identities are not taken into account in therapy; this increases the client's risk of harming herself and/or others, and means that the client is unlikely to significantly improve.
- Practitioners wanting to seek funding for their clients through the NHS are likely to require a diagnosis based on the findings from a SCID-D or SCID-D-R.

Key questions that may be asked prior to full screening are:

1. Have you lost time?
2. Have you ever found yourself "come-to" somewhere but had no recollection of how you got there?
3. Have you ever heard voices that originate in your head?
4. Have you experienced physical symptoms (for example, difficulty swallowing, talking, or moving) where a known cause has never been established?

Assessment and diagnosis may involve:

1. Assessing the client's level of functioning.
2. Using the Dissociative Experiences Scale (DES).
3. Using the Somatoform Dissociation Questionnaire (SDQ-20).
4. Using the Structured Clinical Interview for DSM-IV Dissociative Disorders to support a funding claim (SCID-D or SCID-D-R).

CHAPTER THREE

Beginning stage of psychotherapy

Stabilisation, containment, and strengthening the host

The beginning stage of psychotherapy is one of stabilisation, containment, and strengthening the client's resources to the extent possible. It is too early to look at trauma. Even though there may be identities wanting to talk about what happened to them, at this stage this can be dangerous. This is because it can be too much for the host to manage and can result in an increase in self-harming, suicide attempts, increased drinking, worsening of an eating disorder, or some other harmful behaviour. I explain this to all the identities through the host very early on in therapy.

In this initial stage, psychotherapy needs to focus on strengthening the host so that eventually the trauma events can be shared amongst all of the identities. When clients first attend therapy, there is likely to be a lot of intrusion from one or more of the identities who are stuck in the era and at the age when the trauma took place. This means that current events remind the identities of past trauma, causing these memories to be triggered and partially relived. The host may experience some of the alters' felt experiences, often anxiety, or she may lose time. However, the host dissociated from the original trauma in order to be able to cope with the feelings at the time and therefore has never had to fully realise all that has happened to her. The ego strength of the host therefore needs to be sufficiently robust in order for her to be able to learn to cope with the memories the alters desperately want to share (Ringrose, 2010). Hence, initially, therapy work is restricted, as far as possible, to working on everyday topics, for example, day-to-day living with DID, current relationships, and work issues.

Drawing the client's social map

In the beginning weeks I am trying to build up a picture of the client, her level of support, and what she is able and unable to do. At this stage, I will take several sessions to draw a social map of everyone that the client has ever known and ask her to place herself in relation to these people. This activity helps me to gauge how much support the client receives outside of therapy. I can also intuit more information about the alters. Often they have different feelings about their current social contacts from the host and although in the very early sessions I will not comment on this much, it is useful to observe. This gives an indication of the level of internal conflict, as well as in whose presence the host may become unstable.

Helping clients have a greater continuity of experience

In the beginning stage in particular, strategies aimed to support the client to gain clarity and greater continuity of experience are also useful. For this reason, I type up detailed notes of the client's session and offer to send them via email. I do not do this as a matter of course because sometimes the host may not be ready to hear what has happened in therapy, for example, in cases where an alter has spoken about abuse. The host may also become overwhelmed if she receives too much information and has no-one with whom to process it. This, therefore, depends on the content of the session, the client, and the stage she is at in therapy. Nonetheless, if an alter was present for part of a therapy session, the host(s) may have no memory for a chunk of it, and where the host(s) is concerned about what happened, this information can be shared at an appropriate time. Throughout therapy I am aiming to increase awareness, communication, and cooperation between all of the identities.

Confirming the client's reality

In addition, it is important to confirm the client's reality because she tends to have learnt to distrust what she thinks and feels (Ringrose, 2010). Perpetrators will often have repeatedly confabulated accounts and may, for example, have told the victim that the abuse was her fault, or they may have denied that the abuse occurred altogether, or minimised it in some way. This is partially because abusers need to minimise and justify the abuse to themselves and their victim, in order to be able to perpetrate the crime. This can lead any victim to question what has happened but these clients tend to have been abused on several occasions, often by several abusers and over a period of time, making it extremely common for them to begin to question their experiences, especially as they too want to deny that it happened. Further to this, the abuse often began in the client's childhood, when she would have had a reduced capacity to assess what was happening and why. Where abusers report to children that this is your fault because you have been naughty, children are more likely to believe this and come up with their own explanations to support the perpetrator's claim.

Aside from the above, clients will be unclear about what is real and what is dreamed, or imagined. There are several explanations for this. First, one of the primary symptoms of DID is depersonalisation, which causes the client to feel detached, unreal, distant, fuzzy, and so forth, thereby mimicking a somewhat dream-like state. This arguably encourages the client to put experiences down to dreams. Second, many of these clients have been drugged, or plied with alcohol, prior to the abuse, making it harder for them to recall events. Third, clients tend to have adopted strategies at the time of the abuse in order to try to minimise the trauma. Hence, they have often reported trying to distract themselves with thought tasks, for example, by chanting songs in their head, or counting. They also tend to have shut their eyes, or done everything possible to pretend that the abuse was not happening, or to try to lessen its impact. All of these actions impede processing at the time and encourage the client to question the reality of an experience. Fourth, the dissociative process means that the host has denied that the abuse occurred, the abuser may have confirmed that "the abuse did not happen", and even on occasions where the host is confident that the abuse occurred, she may have told a parent and not been believed, and this process may have been happening over a number of years.

This fosters uncertainty about what is real and coupled with the client's amnesic episodes makes for a very confusing existence.

It is therefore important that you do not ask clients with DID what they are feeling when they are remembering or recounting something bad. For them, you may be questioning their reality of what happened. Clients with an abuse background have had a lot of their reality denied. For example, they have been told "I am abusing you because I love you", not "I am doing this because I am wanting to" (Ringrose, 2010: 127). Although everyone experiences events slightly differently, I use my feeling response (transference) to the clients' accounts as a measure of how they may be feeling and report this back to the clients. I spend a lot of time stating how I would feel if I had experienced the events they are narrating, thereby striving to confirm their reality, or something that is approximate to it. Stating that I would be angry or sad if the event had happened to me, helps the hosts to get in contact with their own dissociated feelings.

However, it is important that when clients talk about their experiences, practitioners use the clients' own language as far as possible and do not go beyond what the clients have said when reflecting their disclosures back to them. This approach reduces the likelihood of the therapist implanting false memories, or that memories will be iatrogenic as it is known. This has been one of the major criticisms about some aspects of trauma work but one which can be easily avoided by taking this approach.

Congruence in therapy

Related to this is the importance of being congruent. Clients with DID have strong antennae and can generally pick up the therapist's dilemmas, problems, distractions, and so forth. For example, if the client asks me if I am okay, I am congruent about what is going on for me; I do not go into detail but I feel the client needs to know she can trust what I am saying to be true. A respondent from my study was asked by one of her first clients if she was feeling unsure about whether she could work with the client, or be able to help her. The practitioner was feeling reticent about the task at hand but her admission of this to the client meant the beginning of building trust between the two of them. In this case, the practitioner admitted that although she did not have all the answers yet, they would find them together (Ringrose, 2010).

Issues specific to contracting

Many therapists recommend making contracts with clients early on in their therapy (e.g., Putnam, 1989). I have a standard contract that I give to all clients (not just those with DID) but I will also talk through verbally further issues with clients with DID. I inform clients about what the consequences will be for breaches to the contract and also outline my availability and its limitations (see under boundary guidelines).

Safety issues

One of the main additional issues I cover when working with these clients concerns safety—to me, the client, and the environment. I state clearly that all feelings are welcome but that these must be sufficiently contained so that there is no harm caused to myself, the client, or the environment during the session. Where an angry alter has needed a space to vent, I have, with some clients, scheduled a session in advance for this purpose. This has meant that I can ensure their appointment does not coincide with another therapist using the room next door. On occasion, I have had angry alters storm out the consulting room or shout and I would not want another therapy session adversely affected by the noise.

Where evident, I talk about aggressive behaviour and self-harming outside of sessions, too. In relation to the former, aggressive behaviour has often arisen because an alter sees this as a means of protecting herself, or one or more of the identities. Talking this through with the alter concerned and giving her other strategies to support the host is useful because often the host does not want this form of protection and can feel quite ashamed and embarrassed by angry outbursts from a young, or teenage, alter. For example, I had one couple come to a joint session where the husband informed me that their relationship was all but over because an angry teenage alter was intent on destroying their marriage by being rude and unpleasant to the husband. The alter was behaving in this way because she believed the husband would eventually abuse one of the identities.

Regarding self-harm outside of sessions, I state that I understand that this sometimes happens but that a goal is for us to eventually understand why, and for the host(s) and alter(s) to find other ways of coping without harming the body. I say this to the host and mention that I am aware that other identities are likely to be listening. I also check out that the host takes care of their wounds, keeping them clean and, where necessary, either uses butterfly stitches or visits a medic for suturing.

In addition, I ask that the host always be the one that comes to therapy and leaves therapy because it is unlikely to be safe for a young child alter to leave alone. Also, eventually, I want the host or hosts to be in executive control outside of sessions all of the time, or until the alters are sufficiently able to manage the outside world without problems. Therefore, I have sometimes found it necessary to orchestrate a switch from alter to host at the close of session. Where a switch from host to alter occurs in session, I will explain to the alter that I will call back the host a minimum of ten minutes before the end of the session. Before orchestrating the switch, I will find out from the alter how she feels about the switch back because she often does not want the switch to occur and a battle can ensue following the session, if this is not worked through prior to the host leaving. I let the alter know that she can return to session in the future and find out what she is going to do once the switch back to the host is orchestrated. At these times I often suggest a task she can complete so she can be busy for a while, particularly if she has been talking about something traumatic. This is because in fostering her well-being and ability to cope, I am assisting the host. The host will experience some of the feelings from the alter and I want to do all I can to settle the entire system. In orchestrating a switch, I literally say goodbye to the alter and call out the host's name. There is usually a moment where the client shifts position in her chair and then returns, often with a headache. I explain, if she does not know, that a switch occurred and then help the client to ground herself back in the room (see below under "The grounding technique").

Ensuring identities are accountable for their deeds

I also ask that the alter who writes, phones, or does the deed, makes herself known, and is accountable. Putnam (1989) notes the importance of alters accepting the consequences for their behaviours by not leaving the spot and handing the problem or mess over to another identity to sort out. He uses the example of an alter who drinks heavily and leaves the headache to the host.

Building a support system for the client

A further issue regarding contracting is to think about which outside agencies may be brought in to further support the client if necessary and what procedures can be put in place if the client needs in-patient support. Making links with other professionals whom you can call upon in times of crisis is helpful. I have a couple of therapists who are able to support clients in my absence.

However, forging links with community mental health teams has proved more problematic for me. Unfortunately, my experience of working in private practice in Yorkshire, England, has been such that where I have informed a psychiatrist of his patient's attendance in private therapy, the client has been told to choose between seeing her community psychiatric nurse or seeing me. I have been given several justifications for this. First, I have been informed that the client is not ready for psychotherapy because she is too unstable. The medical professional involved fears that therapy may exacerbate the client's problems causing her to mistakenly defer therapy until such time when she feels it will be right. This fear is understandable and justifiable. Where therapists work with trauma issues too soon, clients are likely to become more unstable. However, for some clients the time never seems to be right. For these clients, their symptoms seem to be held in limbo for years with drug treatments, and underlying issues are never addressed. The distress thus continues and often clients become dependent on the health service for protracted periods of time.

Second, I have been told that some clients cannot manage a relationship with the nurse and the psychotherapist because having both professionals involved is "too confusing" for the client and creates a "conflict of interest" between the nurse's goals and that of the psychotherapist. However, I have worked in hospitals alongside nurses in multi-disciplinary teams and whilst the relationship between nurse and psychotherapist can be difficult at times, judging by the widespread adoption of this working practice, it is the preferred approach. I therefore fail to see how this should be different in the community. On the face of it, there is no logical reason why clients cannot have a good relationship with a nurse and a psychotherapist. However, I am not a nurse, I would never perform nursing duties, and as far as I am concerned, my role is very clear and need not create a conflict of interest with another professional. Regrettably, almost undoubtedly partly due to funding, local access to NHS psychotherapists is so rare that I can only presume that nurses are performing psychotherapists' duties and that the conflict occurs because where a private therapist is involved, there are two practitioners working "psychotherapeutically". I eagerly await to see the impact, if any, that the registration of psychotherapists will have on this practice.

Therefore, at the time of writing, I do not contact psychiatry as a matter of course when clients first attend therapy. Instead I talk through all of the options with clients and leave the decision as to who is involved in their care team up to them. I loathe that clients are forced into this position. The consequence has been that some clients lose their community nurse, some lie, or do not tell the medical profession about my involvement and most are managed by their GP and myself without a psychiatrist being involved. Where in-patient services are needed in a hurry, clients are then forced to go to accident and emergency, which is far from ideal but the quickest route to in-patient services, or a psychiatrist. I do, however, always notify the client's GP when therapy begins and liaise with them.

Where psychotherapists are able to work alongside the community mental health team, there needs to be an agreement made between clients and practitioners about what information remains confidential to the therapy room and what is shared with outside parties.

A further valuable source of support can come from the client's family or friends. At some point early on in the therapy relationship I will talk to the client about the possibility of bringing a partner, relative, or friend to therapy. I leave the decision to her but this can be beneficial to all parties. As her therapist, I can ask about the problems the multiplicity is causing in day-to-day living and gain a greater level of insight into how the client functions at home. A family member or friend can learn about dissociation, which can bring a sense of relief as she sees that her relative's condition is shared with others, and something can be done to support the client. The relative, or friend, can also help by identifying triggers to switching; can be taught how to orchestrate a switch; and can remind the client of coping strategies at times when she may have forgotten them. All of these elements may relieve some of the stress and tension that tends to have built up in the client's relationships with others, particularly those living with her.

Boundary guidelines

Building a therapy relationship may take longer with these clients because of the level of disruption that they have typically undergone during and since their childhood. A key element to get right in the therapy relationship is the boundaries between client and therapist. It is important that these are made clear and adhered to, providing the client with a level of safety and containment. It is during the beginning stages of therapy that clients learn a lot about what you will tolerate and accept and what is strictly out of bounds. Consistency and predictability are paramount.

Time boundaries

Strict boundaries to the therapy relationship are even more vital for the client with DID because their background has usually been filled with broken ones. However, clients often want to stretch time boundaries, pushing therapists to the limits in this respect, as they strive for more contact between sessions. This is most evident when the identities vie for time in the therapy session. Where therapy is only one hour a week and there are several identities, all wanting to be heard, there can seem like there is never enough time for everyone. This can create conflict between the identities and where possible clients attend more than once a week, or may have longer sessions. In the case of the latter, these are, however, prearranged. As a general rule, I do not allow sessions to run over our predetermined time.

Since these clients pose a high risk of suicide attempts and self-harm, some practitioners get drawn into seeing the client on extra occasions because they fear that if they do not, then the client will self-harm, or attempt suicide. Whilst this fear is completely understandable, what can happen is that the client may learn that the therapist's boundaries will be broken if the client gets very upset. This can result in more crises in the long term, rather than less, as the client strives to see more and more of the therapist.

Managing separation anxiety

Since clients with DID have nearly always had very disrupted attachment relationships, they often fear abandonment and suffer from separation anxiety. In an attempt to alleviate this, when I am away, on occasion, I have left a message for clients in order that they can replay it in my absence. I have also lent clients a teddy bear from a collection that sits in my consulting room, which they return following my absence. This can help young alters keep in mind that the separation is not permanent and that I am returning. Whilst my experience has been that most clients do not take up the opportunity, I do nonetheless ask the clients if they wish to see another therapist in my absence. I give them the opportunity for them to meet before I go away and I leave them with details of how this person can be contacted just in case.

Lastly, occasionally an identity has contacted me between sessions because she fears that she has said or done something "bad" in session. In these instances, I often send a one-line text stating that I am not offended or upset and that I will see her as usual at their next appointment. This can stop the worry going around on a spin-cycle gathering momentum until his next session.

However, there is a fine line between a reassuring one-line text and being constantly bombarded by texts or emails. Often this may be about the host not taking care of a child alter who is distressed. You would not leave a five-year-old child alone for the weekend without having a sitter. This is the same for some child alters, where the host may need reminding of her parenting duties at these times.

Teaching clients how to cope with strong emotions

Clients with DID often struggle to know how to take care of themselves, particularly emotionally. They are unlikely to have had their emotions regulated by a supportive caregiver and thus feel easily overwhelmed, which is compounded by a lack of skills to cope and ways to self-soothe. One of the first priorities is to help the clients regulate their emotions in a different way to self-harming or dissociating (assuming the trauma incidents have ended, see below).

One of the main functions of dissociation is to prevent the host from having to deal with unpleasant feelings. The host simply wants them to go away. However, if they want to stop the dissociative process, it is imperative that clients increase their tolerance to unpleasant emotions and usually anxiety and sadness in particular. In order for the identities to heal, they will need to experience the trauma they dissociated from and, in order to do this, they will need to learn to manage their anxiety in a different way to switching out and leaving the pain to another identity. I therefore teach the host ways to help herself and her identities cope when she feels anxious. I often begin by educating her on the fight, flight, and freeze response because this helps the identities understand their body's response to fear and that it will end. However, it is important to bear in mind that this talk has to be pitched at a level where all the identities can understand.

Managing anxiety

In addition, giving the clients skills to practise when they feel anxious is useful. In the resource and information section at the back of this book I have included detailed material that can be used to help clients to manage anxiety. Together we draw up a list of things that the clients can do to try to help calm themselves down. When the clients first notice anxiety, I begin by asking them to slow their breathing. As the anxiety often relates to past trauma, I ask the hosts if someone is afraid. I encourage them to reassure whoever is scared by reminding her that she is safe now and that nothing bad is happening currently but that the feelings relate to a bad memory that will pass. If clients begin to look like they are getting anxious in sessions, I encourage them to practise sitting with the feelings. I comment on the fact they have started to calm as soon as I notice, this helps them to learn anxiety passes and I give them lots of praise and encouragement for coping in this different way. If clients look like they are becoming overwhelmed I will use the grounding technique to ground them back into the room (see below).

Young alters may need a safe place to go to when times feel scary. I make a plan with the host beforehand so that everyone knows what to do to help little ones at stressful times and we write the plan down. Sometimes I encourage young alters to build their own room with the help of the host. I ask them what colour it would be, what objects would be there, and who else may be in the room. Also, creating an imaginary room lined with mattresses may be helpful for alters to go to instead of harming the body (Ringrose, 2010).

Coping with sadness and anger

We also draw up a list of things for clients to try in order for them to soothe themselves and vent anger in particular. It is better if the list is written down with the clients in session, as initially they often forget what to do in the moment. Examples of soothing activities for child alters are taking a bubble bath, reading a children's story, watching a children's programme, or time in bed with a favourite teddy. Exercises for venting anger include smashing bottles at the bottle bank, singing along to loud music, or taking physical exercise, for example, going for a trudge, preferably somewhere quiet where there will not be other people. Clients will sometimes experience overwhelming feelings and knowing what to do with them fosters a belief they can be more in control. I tend to do this work with the host but occasionally I will talk directly to alters if they present in therapy. Further examples are outlined in the resource section at the back of the book.

Journaling or keeping a diary of thoughts and feelings, as well as drawing, can provide ways for the identities to relieve themselves of some of the material between sessions. Aside from this benefit, the host often wants to pretend the other identities do not exist. By encouraging them to journal, this is proof to the host of the identity's existence and may help an alter to vent, or begin to talk to the therapist.

The grounding technique

If the client looks like she is becoming overwhelmed, I ground her in the session. I do this by snapping her into the current reality by saying her name firmly, clapping my hands, or banging the consulting room door. I ask her to change her position in her chair in order that she is sitting on the edge of the seat. I get her to focus on the contact of her bottom on the seat and to focus on the floor underneath her feet. I ask her to accentuate these feelings by rocking her feet forwards and backwards from the heel of the foot to the tip of the toe. I then ask her to bring her shoulders up to her ears and follow this by pushing her shoulders back down to the floor. I end this physical grounding exercise by getting her to roll her head around in two or three circles in both directions. If the client is still looking distant I will walk around the consulting room and talk to her about what her plans are for later in the day, which helps to navigate her back to the current situation.

If clients become anxious outside of the session, I encourage them to distract themselves by labelling everything around them that begins with a particular letter in the alphabet, or alternatively, I get them to count backwards from one hundred in threes. Strategies that can help clients ground themselves back into the world now involve them focusing on things outside of them. For example, I will encourage them to focus on the wind in their hair, or the sun on their face, people in the street, displays in shop windows, and so forth. Further strategies are found in the resource section.

Fostering listening to and taking care of physical needs

Clients often need to be reminded to look after their basic physical needs. Rather than listen to what they are feeling and deal with the consequences of either not being able to cope with the feeling, or not being able to do anything with it, clients tend to ignore any wants and needs altogether. This is particularly true for clients who were neglected. These clients may forget to eat when they are hungry, or drink when they are thirsty. They may also not allow themselves to drink, eat, or hang on for hours before going to the toilet as forms of self punishment.

Identities also need to negotiate to go to bed and get up at regular times. There are often problems around bedtime, sometimes this is due to an identity punishing herself through sleep deprivation, or alternatively, it may be due to one or more alters keeping her up because late evenings or night times are the only time she is allowed to express themselves. Where the host fails to give the alters any freedom of expression during the day, one or more alters may take over the limelight when the host feels sleepy, disinhibited through alcohol consumption, or numbed with psychotropic drugs. I therefore talk to the identities to arrange time for them to be allowed out to do their own activity. However, it is usually necessary in the early days to talk about what the identities are allowed to do and what they are not. For example, child alters are not allowed out alone after dark. Aside from cases where there are too many identities, I tend to allow all alters time to draw or write and I encourage the host(s) to work out with each identity what their needs are and how these can be best met. Where there are too many alters to have time out individually, this can be arranged through having an in-house nursery with older alters acting as in-house child-minders. I also mention that whoever does the deed, accepts responsibility and all consequences for it. This usually ensures that identities are less likely to misbehave.

The host often wants to absolve responsibility for day to day living tasks, she wants to be taken care of and not be bothered with having to look after herself and her alters. The responsibility of self care and of caring for the younger alters needs to be continuously handed back to the client and praise given for her efforts.

Challenging faulty beliefs

Typically the host and one or more identities do not believe they deserve care. They have learnt they are "bad", "useless", "stupid" people, or something similar and that they should be punished, often relentlessly. These thought processes tend to stem from an external abuser, who has told them these things over a protracted period of time. However, sometimes, these messages are internalised and adopted by a persecutory alter who carries on the persecution of the host and/or other identities long after the original persecution has ended. The persecutory alter sometimes does this under the mistaken belief that she is protecting herself, or one or more of the identities from further abuse from a persecutor. By identifying with the aggressor, she aims to convince the original persecutor that it is not she who is weak but one or more of the other identities, thereby intending to save herself from future abuse. Another explanation may be that she wants to toughen up the other identity or identities in order to try to prevent further abuse. Lastly, a persecutory alter may persecute other identities because she resents being the one who was left to experience all the bad events, so that other identities did not have to (Putnam, 1989).

Alters may also repeatedly push away people who offer help by being unpleasant, rude, aggressive, or they may outwardly obstruct the therapy process. This tends to occur because one or more identities will have been let down by people before and will be expecting to be let down again. In this respect, it is the opposite of the saying "it is better to have loved and lost, than never to have loved at all". The behaviour is thus performed in order to prevent an attachment that the identity assumes will turn out badly.

In further cases, it was not just what was said that led the client to feel she is "bad" but how the client was treated during childhood. Hence, clients have reported sleeping in the coal bunker, porch, garage, or shed because they were locked out of the house. Similarly clients may have been denied meals, whilst other members of the household ate. Clients, who tended to be young at the time, look for a justification for the neglect and ill-treatment and assume they are bad.

The reason for the persecution needs identifying and any faulty beliefs challenged, in order to work towards prevention of current punishment and greater collaboration amongst the identities. In the case of working with persecutory alters this often happens directly, that is, not through the host. I think this is because the alter is too strong for the host to contain. However, I will talk to the other identities about what has been discussed and explain the reasons for the persecutory behaviour because I want to foster an understanding amongst all of the identities and encourage them to get along. This will not happen if identities do not like the alter because she is so persecutory.

Where there is no persecutory alter but the host just "knows" she is bad, I will enquire what she felt she did to deserve this label and the current punishment. When working with current beliefs of this nature, I may encourage the host(s) to challenge these beliefs by asking herself what someone else would think in the same circumstances—would someone else share the same beliefs? Often there are double standards with one rule for herself that is harsh and punishing and a much more forgiving rule in respect to other people.

I often take a cognitive behaviour approach to challenge clients' black and white thinking. For example, these clients often categorise people into all good, or all bad, stupid or clever, angry or calm, and so forth, and sometimes this results in an alter carrying all the "bad" emotion or attributes and then being criticised for it. Identities can be encouraged to get along better if they learn that people are sometimes calm and sometimes angry, that people now and then make mistakes but at other times get things right but that all of these behaviours are part of who we are. This can also reduce the likelihood of one alter being alienated by the other identities because of her "bad" emotion or attribute.

Tempering empathy

Likely due to a further by-product of ill-treatment, these clients find empathy for themselves almost impossible. This means that empathy from the therapist may be too much for the host(s) or one or more of the alters to tolerate and can result in the client self-harming if an identity feels that the care is not deserved. Therapists may therefore need to temper their empathy and nurturing until they are convinced that the client will not be overwhelmed (Ringrose, 2010). Lamagna and Gleiser (2007) state that trauma survivors struggle as much with feeling positive affect

as they do negative. Also, experiences of care and closeness in therapy
may trigger a self-loathing for having dependency needs, or may bring
about intense grief in now receiving what was rarely given in childhood (Lamagna & Gleiser, 2007). What is helpful is a lot of praise and
encouragement for the client's endeavours and comments on how well
she is doing.

Talking through the diagnosis

Talking through the diagnosis takes time and I wait for the client to ask
what she needs to know, rather than risk saying too much and worrying
her. I explain that dissociation is a way of coping with overwhelming
feelings, which for the host is like logging off, or shutting down from
an experience that is too painful to face. I may describe how alters come
along to protect the host from trauma. This can help the host to begin to
think about the alters in a more positive light because not only did she
create them but they have served to shield her from some of the feelings
connected to trauma experiences. A key message to get across is that
although there are these identities, there is only one body and harm to
it by one identity means harm to everyone.

I have also used an analogy of the body representing a house shared
by many identities where each alter may live in different rooms of the
house. Some of the rooms may have the door open, where there is communication amongst the alters, and some may have the door firmly
closed, where there is no communication or only muttering can be
heard. This can be extended to include how some alters can reach one
another, through interconnecting doors, whilst others cannot.

I will also talk to clients about the internal struggles they may have
had with a parental figure who was, on the one hand, relied upon to
provide food and shelter but, on the other, was frightening and abusive.
I explain how this can result in people needing to split off parts of themselves in order for them to cope with the conflicting feelings but remain
in the same environment.

Understanding the dissociative process with clients

Helping clients to understand the dissociative process is one of the
beginning stages in their learning to prevent dissociating altogether.
When working with one of my first clients with DID, I talked to her

about how sometimes she seemed to be fully with me but at other times appeared to have drifted away. I used the analogy of her going up and down in the lift. I said it was as though we both started together on the ground floor but then sometimes she would take the lift, occasionally straight up to the top floor, which we began to call floor ten. Sometimes this would happen with little warning but at other times she would go up more slowly and she, or I, seemed to have a level of control over what was happening. We spent a lot of time looking at triggers to what sent her up in the lift, ways to prevent it, and ways to bring her back down to the ground floor afterwards. If I noticed her begin to drift away, I would make a loud noise—typically banging the consulting room door—in order to keep her with me. If she went straight up to the top floor without me being able to keep her with me, I would ask her to look in her pocket where she would find her keys. Her keys represented something from her current adult life which brought her back to me as the adult she was, not the seven-year-old girl who was abused. This was paramount at the end of the session. I realised that without this, she was not safe. On one occasion, her child alter was found wandering the corridors of the hospital unable to return to the ward she, as host, had been living on for the last three years. Whilst I took responsibility initially for helping her stay with me, eventually she learnt to do this herself as she began to understand herself better. Therapists have reported using several techniques in order to try to keep the host in the room. Smelling scent markers, clapping hands, switching lights on and off, going into trauma events, and coming back out of them again, followed by grounding clients, are a few strategies the therapist can try if the client starts to feel or look as if she is floating off in a dissociative trance (Ringrose, 2010).

* * *

Summary

Key elements and issues in the beginning phase of therapy

- Stabilisation, containment, and strengthening the host's adult ego is paramount.
- Where trauma experiences have stopped, I aim for clients to face difficulties without dissociating.

- Creating a social map provides information about the client's level of support at home and gives clues as to which relationships may lead to conflict between the identities.
- Providing notes on therapy sessions can help clients have a greater continuity of experience.
- Confirming the clients' reality by expressing how you would feel in the situations they are sharing helps clients to accept that their feelings are justified.
- The therapist's congruence encourages clients to learn to trust them.
- Contracting issues centre on the safety of the identities; concerns about confidentiality where outside organisations are involved; and problems managing boundaries.
- Clients usually need to be taught how to cope with strong emotions by sitting with them in session. Grounding and distraction techniques inside and outside of the therapy room can help with this.
- Clients may need encouragement to learn to listen to their physical needs and take care of them.
- Challenging faulty beliefs means that clients update their understanding of past events to those based on adult evaluations. This can improve relationships amongst the identities.
- The therapist's empathy may need to be tempered because it may be too much for the client with DID.
- Talking through the diagnosis helps clients understand their difficulties and how they arose.
- Helping clients to understand the dissociative process is the first step to them beginning to have some control over it.

CHAPTER FOUR

Middle stage of psychotherapy

By the middle phase of therapy clients will have a good level of understanding of their multiplicity. They will know that they have identities and their approximate ages, and have a limited amount of information about the events that gave rise to their creation, although this will not have been gone through in any detail. They may not know all of their identities but, in the main, they will have learnt methods to manage their emotions in times of crisis and know many of the triggers to them feeling unwell. The host (or hosts) will be more stable and their adult ego will be sufficiently strong to cope with everyday living. Self-harming behaviours and suicide attempts will be significantly reduced. That is not to say that the crises will be over. Therapy in my experience rarely runs this smoothly, and nor is there normally a clear uniform demarcation between the stages. At this stage, however, clients tend to be able to be more productive as less time and energy is taken up just surviving. Clients may be working or parenting more effectively and with fewer crises. Social activities may also increase.

Should material be worked through the host, or through the alters?

There is divided opinion as to whether or not it is necessary to talk directly to the alters during therapy (Ringrose, 2010). The main argument for direct communication with the identities is that it is they who experienced the trauma first hand, whilst the host fled the scene. Therefore, some practitioners argue, it is they who need to process the trauma in therapy, not the host, as otherwise feelings may not be adequately cathected, or worked through. This is necessary in order to prevent future re-stimulation of the trauma. In addition, often the host will state that she does not know what the body is responding to when she becomes anxious or distraught.

Conversely, one of the main arguments against talking directly to alters is that this encourages and maintains the use of the dissociative process. In the beginning stage of therapy and in cases where the client is still being abused, the client's ability to keep dissociating may still be necessary. However, at some point once trauma incidents have ended one of the goals is for dissociative episodes to decline.

A further problem with working directly with the alters, is that the host is ambivalent about her identities. On the one hand, she wants them to appear when life becomes difficult but, on the other hand, she often wants them to just go away. Also, sometimes the host has a phobia of her identities and the trauma they carry and thus does not want to deal with them. However, identities rarely (if indeed, ever) go away on their own. By working with the identities through the host in session, this phobia can be empathically challenged. In addition, a further reason against working directly with the alters, is that by talking with them and bypassing the host, the therapist could be accused of encouraging the host to ignore her identities and foster the pretence that they do not exist.

Whilst the host's phobia of her identities is understandable, by the time that the client comes to therapy she has found that there are lots of disadvantages to dissociation and having several identities. She realises that she has lost time and does not know what has happened during that lost time. Alters are also likely to have done things that the host knows little about but nonetheless feels ashamed or embarrassed about and also has to be accountable for, even though she would not normally behave in this way. Alters may be self-harming and initially the host is likely to feel that this is out of her control. Hence, the alters may be causing a great deal of disruption to the host.

I have come to the point where I encourage the host to do the work as much as possible in order to try to discourage the dissociative process and encourage the host to work with her other identities. In the words of one of my respondents, the number one motivator of the client who dissociates is to manage painful and unacceptable experiences, memories, and behaviours through avoidance (Ringrose, 2010). Whilst I feel that this is necessary in respect to avoiding talking about trauma in the early stages of therapy, avoiding the identities will not help the client in the long run; they need to be addressed and I believe this is the job of the host.

A further reason why I favour working with the alters through the host, when possible, is to teach skills that address the avoidance. The task of the host is, ultimately, to be able to accept all thoughts, feelings, fears, beliefs, experiences, and memories as her own. Promoting skills that increase internal communication and self-knowledge in therapy supports this goal.

In addition, some clients have reported that they find it easier if they do not allow a complete switch and instead communicate between the alter or alters and me. This nonetheless is still very tiring for the host who will frequently report getting a headache in sessions, particularly where there is a lot of communication between the identities.

Finally, the host will also often say that she does not know the answer to a question. However, with a little encouragement she and I can learn a lot. It may take time and patience and I may ask the host to do homework to work out what is happening between sessions. The homework will entail getting the host to ask the identities what they know and ask them to draw or write about it.

However, if an alter comes to session, I do not ignore her. If I think it is material that the host is ready to hear, I will try to bring the host back into therapy. If this is not possible and I feel the material is safe for the host to hear, I will report back to her at the end of the session. However, if I feel the material would be too much for the host to hear at the moment, then I will find out what is going on for the alter, work with her through whatever she has brought, and report back to the host when the time feels right.

Therefore, although my aim is to work with the host as much as possible, my experience is that this is not always possible, particularly where there are many alters. Also, there are often occasions when an alter is highly suicidal and will repeatedly attempt suicide without the awareness of the host. It may be too soon for the host to know and understand all that is going on for the alter actions need to be taken to protect the client from further harm. In these cases, there is some agreement amongst practitioners to try to talk to the alter involved in order to find a way that she can cope in a less harmful way (Ringrose, 2010).

Checking whether the identities are comfortable with trauma disclosure

When young alters come to therapy, they are typically desperate to have their feelings heard. However, I will say that I need to ask the other alters' permission, before I allow them to talk through the host (Ringrose, 2010). I do this because there may be another identity, an internal persecutor for example, who is unhappy about disclosure. If an alter discloses trauma material without permission from the others, this can result in self-harming behaviours and sometimes a suicide attempt as an alter attempts to silence whoever is speaking. The alter who is punishing one or other alters often does this because she has been told that she will be killed if she tells anyone about an abuse incident or similar and she usually does not understand that harm to another alter means harm to her too.

It is therefore important to ask if it is safe to talk about trauma and if in doubt wait. Where there are one or more alters wanting to talk but you are unsure whether this is acceptable to everyone, I ask the host to find out this information. If she is unsure, then I ask to speak to the identity who can talk about what the rules are around talking about things first. Here is another instance where I sometimes talk to an alter directly because I am concerned for the safety of the body. Although some alters may sound very angry or abusive when they first come to session (I have often been told to "fuck off", "piss off", "go away", or similar), the heat usually dissipates fast and it is important at these times to remember that these alters were created as a means of protecting one or more of the identities. The reason behind the need for stopping disclosure is usually easily resolved and therapy can resume with the host speaking more freely.

Fostering communication and co-operation among the identities

Clients with DID will normally have done everything they can to suppress the alters. I encourage them to start paying more attention to one another. The focus of therapy is to encourage understanding, cooperation and collaboration between the identities. Therapy resembles family therapy in some respects. In empathising with X, I need to acknowledge that this may lead to Y feeling angry for example and I will acknowledge their feelings too. The point is not to alienate anyone, no matter how angry or aggressive he or she may present. Lemke (2007) writes that by working towards cooperation and collaboration, the boundaries between the parts become permeable, fostering a greater exchange of information, reducing memory loss and encouraging unity. Practitioners have called the ability of the alters to share their thoughts "co-consciousness" and where they share time in the outside world "co-presence".

As therapy progresses, I ask some of the identities to call on each other in times of need. For example, if an exam is approaching, I may ask another alter to support the host in revising and ask a further older alter to mind the children whilst revision is in progress. All the time I am trying to get the identities working together and supporting one another. Eventually I want the host to become the matriarch of her family and to take on an organisational as well as mothering role but this takes time. In the beginning, I work with the host(s) trying to problem solve with her but all the time I am also encouraging her to find solutions for herself.

Another example may occur when a host has decided she is ready to return to work. In these situations I ask the host to think about what her young alters will do whilst she is working. Similarly a host who meets her first boyfriend will need to think about her young alters if she decides to have sex. As these clients have frequently been sexually abused this tends to be a major issue to consider. The host(s) typically wants to avoid these duties and forgets how to cope when things are difficult. However, it is important to keep reminding her of her role and handing responsibility back to the host.

I also use Putnam's (1989) idea of a bulletin board where alters can post messages about what is going on. Alternatively, I suggest they create a psychological room where they can meet and talk. Alters can be encouraged to work together creating the room in the style and with the objects and so forth they want. This is helpful in terms of the alters getting to know one another and they can find out what happens when they lose time. Slowly the client begins to have more of a sense of continuity of time in her current daily living.

When alters appear to work against the host

The host often does not want to work with her alters because she sees them as working against her—harming the body, getting into risky situations, or doing things that the host feels ashamed about. On the face of it, many of the alters' behaviours can appear self-sabotaging or destructive but they are *always* intended to be helpful. A respondent in my research gave a good example of this when she described how one of her host's alters kept commanding the host to answer the telephone to her father, even though this was now unhelpful because the father was abusive. When the practitioner asked the host to enquire about this with the alter, the alter, stuck in the time in which the abuse took place, had learnt that the way to deal with their father's abuse was to let it happen and get it over with as quickly as possible. This young alter did not know that she now had other options (Ringrose, 2010). Working this through with the host and the alter can thus help prevent further abuse and also improve the current relationship between the identities.

Mapping the alters and getting to know them

As more alters emerge, I ask if they have a name. Sometimes they do but where they do not, we make up something but it is always neutral. Sometimes alters carry the names of abusers or of family members the host or one or more identities has mixed feelings about. Under these circumstances, Lempke (2007) recommends the name is changed to something neutral. All the time therapy is aiming to minimise the conflict amongst the identities. Where an identity carries the name of a family member who is disliked by another identity, or where an identity carries the name of an abuser, other identities will be less likely to want to befriend her. Changing the identity's name makes it more likely she will be entered into the fold.

I will also get the host(s) to draw a map of the identities during sessions (see Figure 1). I always ask her to make the drawing herself—rather than me—because sometimes an identity will take control part way through the process. The map is helpful because it enables everyone to see the relationships between all the known and sometimes unknown identities. From this, it is possible to see who is closest to whom, who may control whom, and who is accessible, and to whom. In the example, the client has two hosts: Jan and Janice, the overlapping shapes represent the fact that there is a level of co-consciousness and

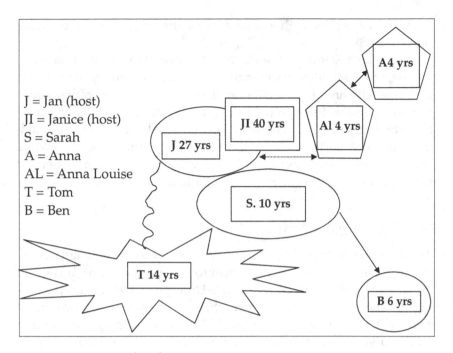

J = Jan (host)
JI = Janice (host)
S = Sarah
A = Anna
AL = Anna Louise
T = Tom
B = Ben

Figure 1. Mapping the alters.

co-presence. Note that Janice is seen as about forty years old, which is older than the client who is the same age as Jan, twenty-seven. This is quite common for an identity to be older than the client, as often she takes on the role of mother. The remaining alters are depicted apart from one another. Anna and Anna Louise are both the same age and are seen as twins, sharing very similar histories and looking identical. Often one or more are out on a limb. Here this is Tom who Jan sees as angry and draws with jagged edges and Ben who is seen as a trouble maker. I comment on these relationships and enquire about those on the outside in particular because often work needs to focus on bringing these identities in closer, so that ultimately all of the identities can work together. In this example, Jan and Janice may be reluctant to bring Tom into the fold because they feel that he is too angry.

The other piece of information I include on the map is the identity's approximate age where this is known. This is helpful because identities need to be addressed in a manner appropriate to their age and the host needs encouraging to do the same. Knowing the alters' age is also informative because it tells us when they were created, thereby providing a clue as to the trauma that may have been occurring at the time, as well as which other alters may be affected by the same trauma (Braun, 1988).

I also ask a host to draw lines to show the level of communication if any amongst the identities. There may be two-way communication shown by a line with an arrow at either end, one way communication which flows only in the direction of the arrow, no connection at all, or a troubled connection as shown between Jan and Tom by the wavy line. Finding out about the alters' issues, problems and functions, all provide useful information. However, this will take time and must be done at the pace of the host in particular but all identities.

Working through trauma events

The final part in the middle stage of therapy is working through trauma events. Communicating with the host to try to work out what is going on for each of the alters is imperative. Unresolved feelings keep drawing the client back to the trauma when it is re-stimulated by current events. These feelings need relinquishing or discharging, but not as a factual description of events given in a detached way. Van der Hart et al. (1993) write:

> Experienced therapists concur that this disorder cannot be completely resolved until these traumatic memories have been successfully processed.

> (p. 163)

Janet (1935, cited in Van der Hart et al., 1993) believed that clients with DID have not "realised" the traumatic event; it is this realisation that eventually brings together the dissociated parts. The alter carries all the time encapsulated memories including body memories and with an intensity that has never been diluted because it has never been shared. The host has avoided trauma incidents and left the alter to deal with them. The host needs to be encouraged to get to know the alters and through the alters' stories, begin to feel some of what the alters feel, thereby removing some of their burden.

Hence, one of the therapist's aims in the treatment of DID, is to assist the client to recover dissociated memories or memory fragments held within each of the alters. Clients with DID are continuously propelled backwards into their past lives, as dissociated fragments of memories are repeatedly re-stimulated by current events. The process of re-stimulation keeps occurring because the material never fully registered at the time, and has not been processed (through the purging of emotions), absorbed and integrated. Van der Hart et al. (1993) assert the necessity of each alter involved in the trauma event sharing his or her experiences with each other alter involved and eventually those not involved in the trauma, so that all parts have the same trauma story but often from different perspectives. Hence, different alters may recount different experiences and views on the trauma event but all must be heard, valued, and respected, and inconsistencies enquired about in a non-judgemental way.

In addition, often during this process alters will have distorted cognitions surrounding the trauma. Typically, the trauma was perceived as "my fault for being bad", or similar. These distorted beliefs need to be empathically challenged. Eventually the host and alters form a chronological life history that the host needs to be able to recount without dissociating or reliving it.

Sometimes clients will have too many alters to keep track of and name individually. In these circumstances, it may be helpful to group the identities by age or level of communication, by shared feeling state, or some other means. In these cases, the pair, trio, or group may be given a name which we can use to identify them and lines of communication and so forth can be used as discussed above.

Drawing a timeline

Prior to therapy clients often do not realise the links between past events; it is as if they are experienced as random thoughts and feelings which are fragmented and make little sense. Building up a sequence of events into a timeline from the client's birth up to the present day thus puts an end to this fragmented existence. This takes a lot of time and patience and clients will go through phases of remembering and forgetting again. It may be that you as therapist hold the story for a while (Ringrose, 2010).

The BASK model

Dissociated memories are made up of four components or levels of experience: Behaviour (B), Affect (A), Sensation (S), and Knowledge (K), or BASK (Braun, 1988). Trauma events can be explored from each of these components or ones that you feel are important. Reporting knowledge of an incident does not mean the identity will be able to draw on their affect or sensations in relation to the experience. For example, these may be dissociated but cause the host to keep getting propelled back to the trauma experience. Working through memories beginning with any one of the BASK components, piecing together the constituent parts and purging the emotions attached to it, takes away the memory's power and stops the cycle of re-stimulation. Usually, I believe clients will have some knowledge of an event or will grasp this component quite quickly but it is typically feelings and/or body sensations that need the most work.

Pacing trauma disclosure

This recounting phase in therapy should be carefully paced. Clients can easily become overwhelmed, resulting in self-harming behaviours and/or suicide attempts. Also, as mentioned above, therapists need to check that all parts are willing for the memory work to take place, in order to ensure that an identity is not punished afterwards for divulging information. Once the therapist is satisfied that it is safe to talk, the host can be encouraged to recount trauma events, but to do this "as if watching from a distance—way far from you" (Kluft & Fine, 1993, p. 142). Van der Hart et al. (1993) recommend that no-one "re-experience their part in the trauma to the full extent but for instance to a degree of 4 on a scale of 1 to 5" (p. 177).

Practitioners also recommend getting a factual description through the host from one alter, about the experiences a further alter or alters have shared. By that, I mean getting the information second or third hand. This has the effect of distancing the host from the trauma incident, thereby reducing its toxicity. Where trauma material carries the potential to be too harmful for an alter to hear, initially sometimes it may be beneficial to suggest that a child alter go to sleep or go to a safe place—perhaps behind a wall—where she cannot hear the trauma (Van der Hart et al., 1993). Whilst the end goal may be for every identity to have the same memories, it is better if this does not happen all at the same time because this can feel too much for the host to contain.

Clients frequently worry about whether they are telling me the truth, about what is real and what is fantasy, or fiction. They are often very reluctant to speak because they fear lying, or fear that by telling me the story it makes it "more real", and they would prefer to believe the trauma were made up. Further to this, there may also be a fear of what will happen if they tell. I reiterate what is outlined in my contract about confidentiality and I tell them I am only interested in getting to what is bothering them; that I am not a judge and this is not a trial; and I am not here to gather facts, just to hear about events as they see them. Regarding the fear of making it more real, I state it either happened or it didn't but speaking about events cannot influence whether they occurred or not. However, talking about them can be the beginning stage of letting go of some of the feelings attached to these events.

A trauma incident will have a finite amount of content to get through. Attention needs to be paid to ensure that clients do not get into this process too late in the session for them to be able to complete the recounting of their incident and have time for some processing after the recounting, as well as grounding work. For some clients I have found that an hour is not sufficient. For these clients, I have contracted to see them for an hour and a half. This needs to be negotiated and I do this on an individual basis. Clients may also appreciate being able to phone for a ten-minute briefing at the end of the day, just in case there are residual problems.

Exploring somatoform dissociative symptoms

Clients are often very clear about where the symptoms are in their bodies (Ringrose, 2010). One practitioner reported:

> An alter sharing pain symptoms can be a window on the alter's experiences. If the host switches and suddenly stands up and paces, grimacing because the pain in her thighs and around her pelvis is so awful, she is telling her story. I know that when she's able to switch back, those pains will abate. But this is a clear beginning to understanding who's carrying the pain, what it's representing and where it came from.
>
> (Ringrose, 2010, p. 100)

I believe somatoform dissociative symptoms are present for one of two reasons. First, they may relate directly to the abuse experience and be held as a body memory, in the alter, the host, or both. For example, one of my clients occasionally has pain in her ankles that relates to an alter being tied during abuse incidents. The second reason for somatoform dissociative symptoms again relates to trauma incidents but to how the alter attempted to defend herself at the time and are thus a re-enactment of a fight, flight, freeze, or total submission response.

The somatoform dissociative symptoms can be seen as actions, which imply there must be an actor, an alter. The alters are stuck in the time-frame within that they were created and sometimes the somatoform symptoms, such as pounding heart, relate to the body's response at the time, in this case perhaps to flee. A further example is that many clients talk about an inability to move that may relate to the freeze response the alter performed during the trauma incident. The reason has to be established in therapy. If it is an alter who is taking over the body, rendering it motionless, then therapy will involve asking who is the actor and what function does the action have? Similarly, when clients cannot speak, not speaking is an action and the questions we need to ask are: who is it who cannot speak and what function does not speaking have (Ringrose, 2010)?

Where clients report somatoform complaints, for example pains in the legs or groin, an inability to swallow, or speak, or move, this can be the starting point of their recovery of a memory and their eventual working through it. These symptoms are due to something in the past that an identity is involuntarily reliving. Alters typically carry the body memories but these too can be worked through with the host and the alter together. It is important to remember that the alters are likely to be very young and will function at a child's level of understanding and capability. Hence, if a child alter comes into session it is important to bear this in mind whilst talking to her and address her accordingly.

Hence, a part of therapy will involve me asking questions to find out more about the client's symptoms. Often to begin with, clients struggle to focus on their complaints because they are so used to trying to ignore them, or avoid thinking about them. I have found that clients use an array of strategies to try to avoid these feelings and sensations (and who can blame them) or try to take them away for a while with something else. For example, many of my clients have an eating disorder and focus on feeling hungry or bingeing and purging instead, or use alcohol or drugs, to numb the pain.

In the beginning stage it is therefore important to look at this slowly but to demonstrate to the client that by staying with the symptoms she can learn to cope and work through them. I let the client know that whilst facing these feelings is scary, by avoiding them she is effectively putting them on hold and they will keep resurfacing at another time. I also talk to clients about how avoidance by switching helps to maintain the dissociative process and this has disadvantages for the host in respect to them feeling out of control and clueless to aspects of their lives. Clients will need plenty of encouragement to begin with because they may feel they cannot cope and will switch or tune them out altogether. Faced with these symptoms, clients often believe that they will fragment and will not be able to pull themselves back together afterwards.

When first beginning to look at somatoform symptoms, I may go through elements of the BASK model in order to try to keep the host focused on what she is experiencing. If the body sensations seem to be too overwhelming to look at straight away, I will get clients to focus on the feelings but by describing them visually. I use this technique as a starting point. I may ask them what they imagine the feeling would look like if they had to draw it. Clients have used a vast array of visual images, for example, black lumps of tar, bright red balls made up of elastic bands, a dead weight, or a boulder inside them, in order to describe their symptoms. Sometimes, if I feel the client needs support staying with the feeling, I will ask about the other BASK components and will often just keep asking "Anything else?" or "Any more"? until I have drained her of all she can tell me. Asking about the client's sensations when she is remembering a trauma incident is also helpful. Hence, for example, I may ask what her heart rate is like whilst she is talking to me about a trauma incident. Encouraging the client to sit with the feelings at the same time as reassuring her that she is safe and that she is simply experiencing a flashback that will pass, will encourage her to stop the dissociative process (Ringrose, 2010). Gradually clients begin to learn that it is safe to feel these feelings and that they can cope.

Clients have reported to me that they feel "emptier of something" after these sessions and will often say that they slept for a longer period than normal. Often these feelings and sensations will be accompanied by memory flashes that I will enquire about too, but sometimes they are not.

Some practitioners enquire about where the feeling starts in the body. Sometimes clients know, sometimes they do not. For example, a research participant reported that her client felt a knocking in his body. The practitioner asked the client to touch the part of the body where the knocking is located and enquired about what happened as a consequence of this. The client reported that the knocking changed in intensity. The practitioner then encouraged communication with the knocking by asking it to increase in intensity if it wanted to answer yes and decrease to answer no. When practitioners communicate in this way with the alter, the host may be too scared to ask the questions himself. However, with agreement from the host, the practitioner can ask instead.

The therapist may then encourage the client to symbolise his experiences by drawing a picture of his body and labelling the parts where the "knocking sits" or the "numbness resides". Drawing pictures like this can result in the host beginning to hear voices. The client mentioned above reported he used to feel like there was arguing in his body all the time but now it seemed as if he was hearing the arguing in his head (Ringrose, 2010).

These beginning stages of communication are gifts in the therapy process because the client finally sees that she can have some control over the sensations and thus begin to feel less powerless. With the beginnings of communication the "knocking alter" can be asked questions that help host and alter alike. "If I do X will this help you to feel better?" Through psycho-education the host learns that these are dissociated parts of herself, that they were created for a reason, and that they serve specific functions. As stated above, these functions will need exploring in therapy (Ringrose, 2010).

This example demonstrates the necessity to start at the client's present level of awareness and understanding. From this point, the host can learn that, for example, the knocking belongs to a dissociated alter of the personality, who is around because she serves a specific function. The host can then learn about her system in the same way as hosts do with alters that talk. Hence, the map of the parts can be drawn, the ages of the alters enquired about, the individual personalities eventually understood and they can begin to learn about one another and learn to work together.

In these instances, it is like the memory has been encapsulated into a physical sensation and has got stuck in the body because it has never had the opportunity to be worked through. There are thus no connections between the sensations or feelings and the part of the brain that processes the trauma event. These pathways need to be connected in order that when the client experiences a given sensation, she can then know why and what the sensation relates to. This usually brings relief because clients can feel like they are under current attack despite knowing that there is nothing in the outside world that is currently causing it. However, sometimes clients report somatoform symptoms that cannot be attributed to one event, or one identity. In these cases, describing the sensation, attaching a label to it, it is usually about sadness, anger, or fear, and soothing it using a global statement which all the identities can identify with, is useful. It is important that these sensations aren't ignored or brushed aside simply because there isn't a definitive understanding, often this comes with time.

Communicating to the client about everything that is observed in the client's behaviour is helpful because the client may be unaware of it. For example, clients sometimes will tell me that they have no knowledge of something but their body will show signs of disagreement. This may be evident in the host whose legs shake vigorously, or who performs some ritualised displacement activity. For example, I had one host who said nothing was happening within her as she was recounting a horrific incident but without me intervening would have torn her scarf to pieces as she pulled repeatedly at its tassels. Clients also tear tissues into pieces, pull their hair, or tell me that they are absolutely fine but shake their head whilst informing me. I had one client who appeared as though she were on a white knuckle ride because she was clinging on to the settee. When I enquired about this she said part of her wanted to run; she was clinging on in order to prevent this from happening. I have also been asked to put a chair in front of the door in order that an identity cannot escape.

Using countertransference feelings (providing these are not your own issues) and reflecting these back to the host in a timely fashion is helpful too because again these may tell the client something about her experience that she may have been unaware of previously. In this way, the therapist can act as a barometer to reflect what is likely to be going on in the client. Clients will often struggle to label their feelings. They may sense their heart beating rapidly, sweat on their palms, and so forth, but may not have associated this with the label "anxiety" and not report feeling anxious. These sensations need to be worked through, labelled, and made sense of. Why is my heart pounding? It is because I am anxious? Why am I anxious and more importantly initially, who is anxious?

Where memories have been shared in this way, I will often discover that the alters will have different feelings attached to the same event or the same family member. For example, one alter may be angry towards mum because he remembers telling her about the abuse and her not believing him, whereas, perhaps the host may want to build a new relationship with mum and move on. This may cause rapid switches of emotion towards the family member and also inner turmoil with one alter feeling angry with another, or hurt by the other's reaction. Hence, where there is a change or shift of emotions in one alter, this has repercussions for all of the other alters, who will be forced to make an adjustment. It is like the rock thrown in a pool; it creates ripples long after it has been thrown. In these cases, work needs to done in helping the host to communicate with the alters, to assist them in finding a way to work through these conflicting feelings.

* * *

Summary

Components and considerations for the middle stage of therapy include:

- Trauma material needs to be worked through because it is this that keeps being re-stimulated by current events.
- Check all of the identities are comfortable with trauma disclosure before starting this work.
- Helping clients understand the dissociative process is the beginning to them learning to control it.
- The overall aim is to foster communication and cooperation between all of the identities.
- When alters appear as though they are working against the host, explore their function; this will help everyone to understand their motives and the identities will be more inclined to accept the alter into the fold.
- Draw a map of the identities and encourage everyone to get to know one another.
- Working through trauma events must be undertaken slowly in order to minimise the risk of the host(s) and/or the alters becoming overwhelmed.
- Exploring trauma events using the BASK model can help identities to relinquish all aspects of the trauma experience.
- Trauma work needs to begin from the host's starting point, which may be with somatoform symptoms.

CHAPTER FIVE

Final stages and integration

Considerations about integration

Integration is the process whereby the host accepts all her thoughts, feelings, and behaviours (past and present) as her own. Therefore, integration means the host needs to let go of the belief that something is "not me". Whilst we can all say, "I wasn't myself when I did that" or something similar, the difference is that the integrated person knows there is only one self. Although she may feel she acted out of character, she still knows and accepts the behaviour was induced by a part of her and that this is always under her control.

Beyond this definition statement, there is controversy as to what integration means. For some practitioners, integration means that the alter personalities become one unified whole. I personally am unsure whether or not this is necessary. I argue that functioning can remain divided, although I have some major caveats (see below).

Kluft (1984) argues that integration is a reasonable goal for the majority of clients with DID, although this will not be achieved by some (Putnam, 1989). Kluft and Fine (1993) found that clients who elect to live as multiples often relapse under stress or if painful material is re-stimulated by current events. They state that most clients then return to therapy for integration work as they have found functional division a myth.

However, if one or more identities relapse when painful material is being re-stimulated by current events, this suggests that there has been insufficient processing of trauma material, rather than this being a reason to justify the necessity for integration. Each identity needs to voice their trauma, purge the emotions associated with it and do the same for each of the other identities until all identities share the same accounts and have the same feelings in relation to these events.

Kluft (1984) also strongly advises clients with DID who are to become parents to integrate. One of the reasons he cites is because alters may exploit or persecute the host's children. Whilst I have encountered similar problems with some of my clients who have DID, I remain unconvinced that this is due to the client not being integrated. Identities tend to persecute the host's children for a multitude of reasons—perhaps because they have mistaken the child for someone else; or because they see the host's children as a threat; because the child alter is unhappy about the attention that the host is offering to the child; or likely further reasons in addition. Nonetheless, whatever the reason, it is the cause of these issues that warrants addressing, not integration. The fact that integrated clients are less likely to encounter these problems is not due to integration per se moreover the extent to which the work has been completed prior to it.

Aside from working through past trauma, a great deal of work needs to be undertaken on strengthening the host's adult ego in order for her to be able to maintain executive control. Part of this work entails teaching the host that having certain feelings is not bad but a normal part of life. She needs to learn to face adversity by coping with all feelings in a way that doesn't involve dissociation. Clients with DID have managed their feelings by absolving themselves of responsibility for them and handing them over to another part. Therefore, new ways of coping need to replace dissociation. Also, in some cases where there are problems with clients leaving therapy to live as multiple selves, it may be that there has been insufficient time spent on the host(s) in particular, to learn new ways to work with her identities without needing to dissociate.

Kluft (1984) further argues that clients need to integrate because of the host's amnesia and because her behaviours are inconsistent, which can compromise her as a parent. However, where the host is amnesic, this suggests that attention needs to focus on why she is amnesic. This is commonly because she is still dissociating and usually because there is a lack of clear communication between host and identities. Finally, where hosts are inconsistent in their parental duties, this can be problematic for the host's child but I would argue that this can be addressed by ensuring that one or two identities adopt the parenting role and ensure there is clear and consistent communication between them in parenting the child. Again, the only relation this has to integration is that these problems will normally have been worked through before integration takes place.

I have come to question the concept of integration, insofar as I do not believe it is an either/or question where clients either live as multiples or as integrated people. I do not have DID and in this respect arguably represent an integrated person but I do have several sides to me and believe I am far from alone in this respect. I imagine that many of us on occasion would say we have a heart that tells us to do one thing and a head that states we should do another. We may also say things like "he brought out the child in me" or we may have to wear a suit in order to "play the part". Hence, in these respects we are all multiple. However, the main difference between myself and someone with DID is that I retain executive control all of the time and always have a sense of knowing who I am, whereas executive control in clients with DID may change from one identity to another as they switch, as will their sense of who they are as individuals.

Therefore, whilst I am unsure about whether complete integration is necessary, I believe it is vitally important to ensure that the host(s) retains executive control and for her to reach a state of equilibrium which is roughly equal to what any one of us experiences when we feel at odds with ourselves. In addition, there also needs to be an agreement of purpose amongst the identities. For example, if the host wishes to attend university but has not worked this through with the other identities and one identity thinks dance is their chosen career, the whole system can become paralysed. However, I see this as demonstrating the vital roles that communication and collaboration play amongst the identities, rather than an argument that all should integrate. Nonetheless, this latter point highlights one of the practical reasons why some clients choose to integrate. They state they do not want to have to switch between alternate personalities in order to be able to relate with all parts of themselves. For some clients this can be hard work (in the beginning stages, this can leave the client with a headache) and time consuming, but for other clients, dissociation is not necessary in order for the host and alters to communicate and decisions can be made almost simultaneously. It seems highly individual. Lastly, one of my respondents had a wonderful analogy to describe how clients can live as multiples. She said they can learn to move and work together to one goal, similar to a flock of birds, with each bird flying independently but also flying in synchrony with their neighbour (Ringrose, 2010).

Whether clients integrate or choose to live as multiples they will typically have to undergo a great deal of work in order for them to reach a level of stability long term. Whether we subscribe to the concept of integration or not, therapy for this group of clients is costly. It will usually comprise of one or two sessions per week, for a protracted period of time, typically taking two or three years to achieve a reasonable level of stability without integration. My experience in the UK has been that therapy is usually funded by the client, or one of their close relatives, at least initially. Hence, for many clients integration may be a luxury they cannot afford. However, once clients improve, they are more likely to be able to get paid work and fund their therapy themselves. In these cases, clients to some extent, can choose how far they are prepared to go in psychotherapy.

Aside from cost, a further disadvantage to integration is the emotional cost of staying in treatment longer, which Kluft and Fine (1993) argue may be too demanding for older clients. Where clients have achieved a reasonable level of functioning, they may struggle to sign up for more work which they may view as reaping little reward by comparison. Also, some clients fear they will lose an ability which one alter carries. For example, one of my clients has a creative alter and she fears that integration will mean that she loses access to this creativity and as she sells much of what she creates, this would mean a loss of income, too. This case highlights the problem which can arise when alters want to retain their individuality without which they fear they will lose their identity and disappear. At these times I find it helpful to talk to the client about the multiplicity in all of us. I have a creative side to me which loves to sing and dance but that has to remain quiet sometimes so that I can perform other tasks. This doesn't mean that my creativity is lost, merely suppressed at times in order that other sides of me can enjoy the limelight or get on with the practicalities of daily living.

These issues need to be considered with the client at an appropriate time. Discussing integration early on in therapy is unlikely to be useful because at this time the alters tend to be unable to see what they share in common and are more inclined to focus on the differences between them.

Work to be completed before integration

Integration occurs at the end of a long process in therapy. Kluft and Fine (1993) state that prior to integration alters need to have expressed their trauma. The Behaviours, Affect, Sensations, and Knowledge (BASK) around the trauma experiences need to have been voiced, discharged of emotion, fully processed, and the histories shared with one another, before integration can be considered. Aside from the trauma work, integration can be fostered throughout therapy in three further ways: first, by advocating a philosophy of pulling together to fight the common enemy of the after effects of trauma; second, by facilitating an equality amongst the alters, where competition is minimised; and third, by encouraging empathy and understanding amongst the alters and thereby fostering a sense of unity. Further to the sharing of histories and the BASK elements associated with the alters' past, where clients opt for full integration alters will need to let go of their desire or need to view themselves as individual entities. Lastly, some clients cling on to alter personalities because by doing so they can pretend that only the alter was abused, they were not. This would need to be worked through with the host(s) in order for her to come to terms with and accept what has happened to her, as well as her alter(s).

Co-presence, fading, and merging of alters prior to integration

Co-presence is where alters share the spotlight, which can mean the sharing of talents and abilities with one another prior to complete integration and thus can be a useful stepping stone to this end. However, there needs to be careful consideration of the impact that this may have on alters not directly involved. Asking if anyone has any objections to this can reduce the risk of some alter unhappy about it mutilating or abusing the body, or attempting suicide. In addition, prior to complete integration, often one or two alters may appear to merge as their need for separateness diminishes, or similarly alters may appear to fade into the background. Whilst these are signs suggesting that progress towards integration is being made, they cannot be taken as a foregone conclusion that integration will be acceptable to all of the parts, even those which appear to have faded for a while. Complete integration requires an agreement from all parts and there will usually be a period of adjustment afterwards.

Finally, Kluft and Fine (1993) recommend hypnosis to be used in order to ascertain whether alters have faded, or are simply shadows of their former selves but may re-emerge. They also outline further fusion rituals involving death and rebirth, for example, which may encourage final integration and mark the passing of multiplicity. Further therapists argue that where there is good cooperation and collaboration amongst the identities, where the identities no longer have any need to live as multiple, most choose not to, and integration in these circumstances can happen spontaneously (Ringrose, 2010).

* * *

Summary

- Integration is the process whereby the host accepts all her thoughts, feelings and behaviours (past and present) as her own.
- The decision over whether clients choose to integrate, or stay multiple, needs to be explored towards the end stages of therapy.
- There is controversy over whether integration is necessary, or whether clients can learn to function effectively as multiple selves.
- Merging, fading, and co-presence are signs that clients are working more cohesively and are suggestive of the client operating in a more integrated manner.
- Integration is possible only after:
  o The identities have worked through their individual trauma and this has been shared amongst all of the identities in the system.
  o All of the identities are able to share their talents with one another.
  o There is a feeling of equality among all the identities, where competition is no longer necessary.
  o The identities have empathy for one another's experiences.
  o Alters can let go of their desire to be unique.

CHAPTER SIX

Considerations for psychotherapy

This chapter begins by outlining some of the main differences to the structure of therapy sessions when working with clients with DID. The second part details some of the problems encountered when practitioners adhere to their therapy approach too closely when working with these clients and mentions some of the therapy approaches specialist practitioners working with DID advocate. The chapter ends by outlining some of the techniques and strategies that can be adopted by therapists and clients which aim to help clients cope with anxiety in particular.

Changes to the structure of therapy sessions

Therapy tends to be long term

Although therapists differ as to precisely how long therapy will be, there is agreement that therapy with these clients will be long term. Coons et al. (1988) suggest approximately twenty-two months, whilst Kluft (1984) argues anything from two to ten years. Therapy is long term because clients tend to have experienced repeated abuse by several people, or suffered from poor attachments, or both, and these tend to be particularly grave in nature and have occurred throughout childhood.

In addition, it may take clients a longer time to establish a relationship and it may take them a while to stabilise, as they tend to come to therapy when they are in crisis. Accepting the diagnosis takes time. Clients need time to accept their alters, there needs to be time for the alters to learn to communicate and begin to support one another, as well as time for them to achieve a way of working together, or where clients choose it, to integrate. Therapy duration is an important consideration for therapists who are considering a career break or retiring in the next couple of years (Ringrose, 2010).

Sessions are usually more frequent at some point

Once the initial relationship has been established, more regular sessions are often recommended. Therapists need to bear this in mind if they work a fixed number of client hours per week. Putnam (1989) argues that an ideal is twice-weekly sessions, occasionally upped to three times per week; without which, therapy may be stalemated and above which, on a regular basis, the therapy relationship may become enmeshed. I have found that with clients in the middle phase of therapy, particularly when we are working through trauma, less than twice a week sometimes results in clients having to carry too much, or there being too much material delivered between sessions in email for us to keep track (see below). It is when clients feel overwhelmed with the amount of material and trying to contain it that problems are more likely to arise. It is at these times that clients' coping behaviours, for example, excessive drinking, cutting, bingeing, and purging, will be more likely to occur. Where only weekly therapy is possible, many sessions may be spent mopping up after the latest aftermath, rather than looking at the underlying causes of the problems.

A longer session length may be necessary

When the host(s) is working through her trauma with the alters, the length of sessions may need to extend to an hour and a half, particularly at times when there is abreactive work. However, longer sessions must be booked in advance, rather than allowed to run over. Whilst I feel that all clients need clear boundaries, these clients do in particular, as often there are young alters who are looking for a full-time parent and will not want to leave at the end of sessions.

Sessions need to be sufficiently long for clients to have time to get into the work, for the work to run its course, and for the client to feel grounded afterwards (Putnam, 1989). Whilst some clients can do this within an hour, others cannot.

Clients with DID can have extremely clear detailed scenes from their past which they may replay (and relive if we are both not careful). It is sometimes as if they are watching or participating in a recording of an incident from their former life. Using a form of self-hypnosis, clients may enter a deep trance-like state from which they recount past trauma. Occasionally, it is as if they are in two worlds at the same time—the therapy world with me, and a second world, one in which the trauma took place, which will usually involve younger identities. Where clients have had insufficient processing time, they may be left stuck partly in the present and partly in the scene which they have been working on by the time they leave therapy. Therefore, it is vitally important that the host is able to play out her scene to its conclusion and that there is time for both host(s) and alter(s) to be debriefed afterwards. I will ensure the alter(s) is settled and may give her a task before she leaves (which often includes doing something pleasant) and I will also ensure that the host leaves grounded and in charge.

Extra work may be necessary between sessions

There is also likely to be more work involved with clients with DID between sessions. Most practitioners recommend close liaising with the GP and any other members of the client's team. This means letters to write and care plan approach meetings to attend and prepare for. There may be crisis calls from other practitioners, which seem to always come on the spur of the moment and typically arrive at a busy time. If I see a client on a Friday and she seems particularly vulnerable, I will offer her the option of up to an hour's therapy on the phone at a fixed time on a weekend. I do this because weekends are notorious trouble spots but I mention I cannot always guarantee this. Also therapists sometimes offer the option for clients to email concerns between sessions, as this helps prevent them feeling overwhelmed with material (Ringrose, 2010). Emails can be scanned but usually not responded to between sessions but instead taken along to the next session and explored then.

Obviously there will be exceptions in respect to appointment changes, or crises. This work all takes extra time and resources which therapists may not be accustomed to requiring.

Changes to the content of therapy sessions: issues and considerations

One therapy approach is unlikely to be sufficient

The guidelines on the evaluation and treatment of dissociative symptoms in children and adolescents, written by the International Society for the Study of Dissociation, state:

> The most successful treatment approach to an individual case is often the most eclectic, with the therapist showing flexibility and creativity in the utilisation of a wide variety of available techniques.

> (International Society for the Study of Dissociation, 2004, p. 122)

The respondents who participated in my research supported this sentiment. In the box below, I have listed all the approaches that practitioners talked about using in their therapy with this client group. There will be others but the point I wish to make is that one approach is unlikely to be sufficient.

Therapy approaches used in the treatment of DID	
Person-Centred Therapy	Family and Systemic Therapy
Cognitive Behaviour Therapy	Focusing Oriented Therapy
Cognitive Processing Therapy	Hypnotherapy
Dialectical Behaviour Therapy	Sensorimotor Therapy
Eye Movement Desensitization and Reprocessing (EMDR)	Transactional Analysis (particularly the ego state model)
	(Ringrose, 2010)

Child development

Aside from the above approaches, several therapists recommend knowledge of child development as particularly important. This is because there are often child alters who come to session and these need to be appropriately addressed and worked with. Child alters may have built up belief systems that are currently unhelpful for the client and these may need to be safely explored. For example, I had one child alter who thought that if she hid and was quiet she would not be harmed because she was invisible, but this carried the potential to leave the host open to more abuse. A further example came from a child alter who could not allow any of the identities to speak in therapy because she believed this would wake the bad spirits who would come and take her to hell.

I do not feel it is necessary for the therapist to diagnose DID from the start. Indeed, I believe it is often unnecessary to diagnose clients with a specific disorder when I am working with them. Commonly I will not know what the client's formal diagnosis may be. Many therapists stumble across their first client with DID and know little about the disorder but can muddle through in the short term. However, for many reasons, it is useful for the therapist to have an understanding of the issues and problems that may be encountered when working with this client group and where possible for the client to be diagnosed before the disclosure of trauma incidents begins.

Managing the pacing and timing of disclosure

One of the main reasons why diagnosis is important is because it is desirable if therapists can monitor the timing and pacing of trauma disclosure. As a person-centred therapist, I was taught that clients talk about what they need to share when they are ready and that this should be monitored and controlled by the client. However, for clients who are multiple, the host may not know of another identity's existence, let alone need to check out if it is safe to speak in therapy. Where an identity discloses against the wishes of one or more of the alters, this can result in self-harming incidents, as one identity becomes angry with another for a disclosure, or attempts suicide, as one identity tries to silence another in the mistaken belief that they do not share the same body. Hence, when working with clients with DID, therapists may need to prevent disclosure by talking to the identities about holding on to trauma until all of the identities are sufficiently strong to cope and all approve of therapy and trauma work.

This highlights one of the problems which can occur when a therapist adheres to their therapy approach too closely. For example, in my person-centred training, I was taught that I should not direct therapy. I learned that if I direct the client to talk about what I feel is important,

I am not fostering an internal locus of evaluation which is necessary to develop the client's self-esteem. Many person-centred practitioners argue that where therapists direct therapy by telling clients what they can and cannot talk about, clients can come to rely too heavily on the therapist or other people to tell them what they need and this will inhibit her psychological growth.

Over the years, I have become sceptical of this doctrine when applied to all clients irrespective of their needs and have changed my practice to adapt my style of working dependent upon the client. With one of my first clients with DID, I thought I had safely managed trauma disclosure by delaying the process until I felt I knew all of the identities and was fairly confident they were all in agreement about trauma disclosure. Nonetheless a male identity slit the host's throat after she had talked about their trauma past. This male identity did not understand that all the identities would die if he killed the host. He believed that by cutting the host's throat this would silence the host and save him. He had been threatened by his abuser that he would be killed if he ever spoke about the abuse. Fortunately my client survived and has no lasting damage except a scar. This is not an isolated case. Margaret Warner (1998) writes of a similar incident occurring in her practice, and I am confident there will have been others. Whilst prevention of such incidents can never be guaranteed, in retrospect, I feel that a slower pace and checking out before each trauma disclosure may have prevented this. I have found that it is very easy to become carried along with the client's desire to talk through all of her trauma quickly in order to get it over with.

Therapy is not individual—the multiple identities need to be considered

It is also helpful for therapists to diagnose DID because therapy with this client group can resemble family therapy, where all identities need to be considered. The therapist's knowledge of the client's multiplicity and the ramifications this has for her in and outside of therapy sessions is helpful.

The role of psycho-education

Education on the management of the client's feelings

Knowledge of DID is also useful because there is a great deal of literature advocating that clients are taught ways to manage their feelings differently, in order that they eventually no longer need to dissociate, cut themselves, or feel there is no option but to end their life. Ideally, it is advocated that this happens before trauma disclosure.

Education on their multiplicity

Often when the host(s) first attends therapy, there are amnesic barriers between the identities who simply experience losing time, or she may have what appear to be random thoughts or feelings which make little sense to her. Where therapists have an understanding of DID this can be used to educate clients, thereby helping them to understand their multiplicity better, which usually brings a sense of relief.

Clients taught to cooperate, communicate, and collaborate with the identities

In addition, the host(s) needs to learn how to cooperate, communicate, and collaborate with her identities, irrespective of whether or not they eventually want to integrate. It is preferable for the therapist to keep promoting this process throughout therapy. Where therapists are unaware that the client has DID, these processes are unlikely to be undertaken and the client may remain stuck.

This is not intended to be a complete list of all the ways that the content of therapy sessions may differ with these clients but is used merely to serve a few poignant examples.

Techniques and strategies

Therapy with this client group also tends to differ because practitioners adopt a number of different strategies and techniques in their work.

Motivational interviewing, working with DID, and eating disorders

I use motivational interviewing in therapy because I find clients go through phases of being very ambivalent about changing some of their behaviours. At these times, I think it is equally important to look at what obstructs therapy, as to what is facilitative. Motivational interviewing is very useful in this respect.

For example, many of my clients with DID also have an eating disorder. Usually, one element of therapy with these clients involves me taking a very practical approach that looks at the habitual nature of the eating disorder. In respect to bulimia, this involves us working together to find ways to break the cycle of being extremely hungry, and then over-eating, followed by purging due to the over-eating. Often encouraging clients to eat smaller amounts of food more regularly and educating them about not becoming overly hungry is a good starting point.

However, through motivational interviewing it is possible to establish what the client finds is beneficial about the eating disorder. For some clients with DID and anorexia, I have learned that they stay hungry in order to distract their mind from abuse incidents and flashbacks. Clients who are hungry all the time tend to fill their head with thinking about food, which works as a great distraction from what they see as more harmful thoughts of abuse incidents. Nonetheless, clients also want to resume eating normally because the eating disorder carries problems of its own, for example, headaches, dizziness, and tiredness, which restrict the client's ability to partake in normal activities. These two opposing forces can keep clients stuck. However, clients can be taught ways to cope with the aftermath of abuse that do not have these drawbacks.

In addition to staying hungry as a means of distraction, sometimes there is something about eating or the sensations following eating which remind the client of abuse incidents which she desperately wants to avoid. Hence, I have had one client who has bulimia who managed eventually to keep her breakfast and lunch down without purging but said she was unable to eat dinner and prevent herself from being sick afterwards. On most occasions she felt panic following the consumption of dinner, irrespective of what it was exactly that she ate or the amount of calories she took in. As we consume food and drink throughout the day, most people's stomachs distend as the day progresses, and therefore it is not uncommon for people to feel thinner on a morning than an evening and for those who are very sensitive to these natural fluctuations, eating on an evening is usually the hardest. Through motivational interviewing, what we realised was that young alters could not bear to feel full because this reminded them of abuse incidents in which they had objects placed inside them. These full feelings were always worse on an evening because they had eaten breakfast and lunch. Understanding behaviours in this way is the first step to tackling them.

Managing anxiety

Many clients with DID have anxiety and panic. I therefore teach clients ways to manage this because eventually I want them to cope without needing to dissociate, cut, or use harmful behaviours, such as turning to alcohol, or excessively controlling their eating.

Clients with DID are often anxious because a young alter has been reminded of an abuse incident from the past. At these times, they will have a fear response to fight, flight, flee, freeze, or totally submit. I explain the main symptoms that the body will experience because often these clients cannot label their feelings. They may also need to carry this list with them to help them to remember the feeling:

- Rapid or difficult breathing
- An urge to run
- Freezing, or an inability to move
- Increased heart rate
- Jitteriness
- Tension
- Sweaty hands
- Chest pain or discomfort
- Numbness or tingling feelings
- Light-headedness.

Breathing and relaxation exercises

One of the techniques I use, the progressive relaxation technique, was devised by Edmund Jacobson (cited in Bernstein & Borkovec, 1973). It is a simple technique aimed at helping clients relieve their anxiety. It is based on tensing and relaxing muscles throughout the body. I have detailed this and further breathing techniques in the resources section under managing anxiety.

Graded exposure

A further technique I have found helpful with clients whose anxiety has resulted in them feeling unable to complete tasks, is graded exposure (Kennerley, 1997). Some clients have stopped doing activities outside of the home because they are fearful that they can no longer cope with even small tasks, such as buying groceries in the local shop. There seem to be several reasons for this. Sometimes this happens when the adult ego strength of the host is poor, or where the adult ego strength is reasonable, but because there are child alters around at the same time, their fear is felt by the host to a degree which makes her feel that her capabilities are too severely compromised to manage. In these cases, I have found that it is possible to strengthen the ego of the host(s) by encouraging her to take on small tasks and build on successful completion of these, until goals are met. Where the feelings an alter has in relation to a task is preventing the host from completing it, I will make suggestions of what the alter can do during these difficult times, thereby relinquishing the host to get on with the task in hand.

Another reason I have found for why clients are struggling with anxiety is because the host may at times disappear for a while, leaving a young alter to cope with adult duties. In this latter case, I will encourage the host to return, but if this does not happen for a while, I will then work with the most capable alter and encourage her using the same techniques. These have to be tailored to suit the capabilities of the alter, who may often be a child.

I want to encourage the identities to face fears, rather than avoiding them by dissociating or using some other problematic coping behaviour. This in itself can be worrying for the client. However, I explain that often when faced with a challenge, we feel that we have to do it all at once but when we have been avoiding doing something for some time, this can be too difficult to face and hence the whole task is avoided. The precise steps I undertake with clients can be found in the resources section towards the back of the book.

Distraction activities

Distractions away from the anxiety-provoking situation can be a useful short-term tool to managing anxiety in a difficult situation (Kennerley, 1997). I always ask clients what methods they have used to try to cope with difficult situations. Often they have a number of things which they have used intuitively but they may forget these coping strategies at the time of need. I therefore get them to write these down on a postcard and keep it with them. We add several other distraction strategies they can try, should they find themselves feeling overly anxious between sessions. I suggest they use one of two basic types of distraction, thought or behavioural distractions. During the beginning stages of therapy, I will sometimes enlist the help of a partner or friend of the client who can remind her of her list at pertinent times.

Thought distractions

Some of the thought distractions I suggest are:

- Count and name all the things in the room which begin with a given letter of the alphabet.
- Describe to themselves or whoever is with them, what they can see, feel, and hear in minute detail.
- Ask them to conjure up a favourite walk and encourage them to go down all the paths in their mind.
- Hear the words to a song in their head and repeat them until the fear has passed.
- Ask them to recall a funny moment or one that gave them pleasure.
- Conjure up a memory of a happy time—perhaps on holiday.
- Think of a category of objects, for example, vegetables and recall one beginning with each letter of the alphabet.

Behavioural distractions

I encourage clients where possible to do something physical if they become anxious. I explain that when we become anxious our body produces adrenalin and that it is useful if we can burn some of this off, and if it distracts us from worrying too, then this is even better. I persuade clients to try different coping strategies. Below are a few examples:

- Go outside and walk in time to music on a personal player.
- Do some gardening or housework, but try to make it more fun by coupling it with something enjoyable. For example, ironing whilst watching a favourite film, or listening to a story on the radio whilst mopping or dusting.
- At the pub, go to the bar or visit the toilet in order to have a short break.
- If a friend pays a visit, suggest you go for a walk around the garden or block.
- Draw or doodle on a notepad when in a meeting.

At a party …

- Offer to hand out the food or drinks in order to distract from worrying thoughts.
- Help in the kitchen with dishing up, or washing up.
- Offer to read to one of the children, or play with them whilst parents are busy.

Coping statements

I also give clients the following list of things that they can say to themselves when they begin to feel anxious.

- I must try not to give in to worry because this will tell the identities that there is something to worry about and it will make us all less able to cope now and in the future.
- I need to take a few slow breaths. It will help if I concentrate on slowing down my breathing.
- I am safe, nothing dreadful is happening now; these are old feelings based on bad memories.
- I have done this before, so I can do it again.
- If I think clearly, I can overcome this.
- If I do this, I will feel a sense of achievement.
- It is better for me to think about what I can do, rather than what I can't.
- This is an opportunity for me to practise coping.
- The more often I cope, the easier it will be for me.
- If I plan what I am going to say or do, then I will feel more confident.
- I am going to look at the things that I can do.
- I can do this.

Basic Cognitive Behaviour Therapy principles

I teach the host(s) some of the basic principles of Cognitive Behaviour Therapy (CBT) because this can help her to see how she may be inadvertently sabotaging her best efforts to overcome problems. I explain about the interplay between thoughts, feelings, and behaviours and how each one influences the other. For example, how we think influences how we feel, which in turn influences how we behave. I illustrate this with an example.

The host visits her mother at her home. They are sitting having tea and chatting when the door bell rings. Unbeknown to the host this reminds a young alter of an abuse incident. The host becomes anxious and has a feeling of wanting to run.

The first step is for the host to recognise this as anxiety and that it relates to a past event. She needs to reaffirm to herself that nothing bad is currently happening and convey this to the other identities. The host needs to say to herself and the identities, "I am safe, this is anxiety and it will pass." I explain to the host that she needs to parent her identities and soothe them at these times. I encourage her to think of how she would parent anyone who is frightened and adopt the same strategies to help her inner identities. In time, the host begins to know the triggers which cause the anxiety and together we begin to pre-empt problem situations and plan for them in advance.

The role of interpretation

I will also explain that how we interpret an event will influence how we think, feel, and subsequently behave. If the host accepts the anxiety as a sign to fight, flight, flee, freeze, or totally submit, then this will strengthen this connection, making it more likely to keep happening. I therefore explain how events become associated, particularly those which are allowed to by-pass our thought processes. Therefore, if, for example, a client has experienced repeated abuse at a school, as an adult she may become anxious when visiting a school. The trigger therefore is the trip to school, perhaps with her own children. If she becomes anxious and as a consequence stops taking her children to school in order to avoid the anxiety, she is effectively telling herself there is a current problem with visiting schools and these must be avoided. This process keeps the client stuck and provides no opportunity for the fear to be extinguished.

Generalisation of feelings from one situation to another

I also explain about how feeling reactions can generalise, that they can begin by happening in one situation but eventually may be felt in a variety of situations. Hence, in the example above, a client who is initially anxious walking to school may eventually be unable to drive past the school and has to drive a convoluted route to avoid passing the school gates. I thus talk about how behaviours can be extinguished and the role that interpretation plays in this. That is, if we can see the problem for what it is, a fear response to a past event, and that we can challenge it in the current situation, as well as work through the past event, it will eventually disappear.

The example I use to demonstrate how our interpretation influences how we feel and behave is one in which a client is woken in the middle of the night hearing a bang. There are a number of different plausible explanations for the bang.

One explanation may be from a child alter who, reminded of past trauma, fears that the bang signals an abuser coming home and impending abuse. In this case the client is likely to feel anxious and may freeze.

A second explanation for the same noise may be: "That's Jane (daughter) coming home from a late night out." This may mean that the client can reassure and calm the child alter so she can feel relief and with practice will be able to roll over and go back to sleep.

I explain to the host that in the first example, the interpretation of the cause of the bang caused a feeling of anxiety and led to the behaviour, freezing. In the second example, where the same noise was interpreted by the host as non-harmful (daughter arriving home) this can lead to relief and the identities going back to sleep. Hence, these different responses arise through the same event happening—the bang; it is simply how this is interpreted that causes the subsequent reaction. I will mention the importance of listening to the identities' fears, that there may indeed be something to worry about but sometimes our actions are based on the wrong interpretation, one that has long passed and that it is on these occasions that we need to consider their likelihood.

I will also explain that this is a cognitive behavioural element to therapy but that eventually by processing the trauma and purging the emotions attached to it, the alters will become less affected by their past traumas. However, I often need to do both pieces of work, the work on current problems, as well as the work on past traumas, and may do the above behavioural work first if it is too soon for the identities to look at their trauma.

Challenging unhelpful behaviour patterns

Avoidance

As one of the primary coping strategies of clients with DID is dissociation, and dissociation is about avoidance, I talk about the positive and negative effects of this. I explain that avoidance is a very common way of trying to cope with anxiety and that in the short term this seems sensible. However, I explain that by avoiding the feared situations when the interpretation is no longer correct, this results in strengthening the belief that this is something to be scared of doing. This can have the effect of making the feared situation harder to challenge the next time and making it more likely that it will be avoided altogether. In addition, by avoiding fearful situations, there is no opportunity for the fears to be disconfirmed because they cannot be tested out to ascertain whether the anxiety is reliable.

Fortune telling

I talk to clients about their own self-talk. I explain that what we tell ourselves (usually silently) before facing an anxiety-provoking event can make the feared event worse. Fortune telling is fraught with risks of making things worse and in reality we cannot possibly know what will happen beforehand. Predicting harmful outcomes only serves to heighten anxiety. I encourage the host to stay open-minded when facing potentially anxiety-provoking situations. I ask clients afterwards if it was as bad as they imagined; it often isn't and this provides important learning for them.

Catastrophising

Many anxiety-provoking situations are exacerbated by the way the event is foreseen. Clients fear they will panic; it may be that they will but equally it may be that they won't. Unfortunately if they let their thoughts on the situation run rampant, this is likely to only make their anxiety worse. The client will not know what will happen until the event arises but I encourage her to ask the question of whether, if she does panic, will this be a catastrophe? How will her life change if she panics at the supermarket, for example? What will it mean for her as an individual? How important is it really if some people in the supermarket witness her having a panic attack? What would these witnesses think or feel? The client most likely fears that by panicking in public she will make herself look silly or show herself up in some way, but who would really criticise someone for looking scared? If someone were to say something unkind would that really matter? It wouldn't be pleasant but what value would you place on the person's opinion who mocked you for being scared? Is it important to care what they think? I encourage the client to challenge her catastrophic thoughts in this way, thereby helping her to establish what really matters and what does not.

Black and white thinking and exaggeration

Clients often talk in "all or nothing" terms. They tend to use words like "everyone", "never", "always", "anything", and "everything". I will challenge these global statements with evidence failing to confirm it. For the client who says "I always get it wrong" I will remind her of the times when I know she has done something right and encourage her to do the same. Is it really that she cannot "do anything properly" or is it that she cannot do this or that *yet*, but with practice and time she may be able to? I encourage the client to challenge perfectionism too. Many feel that if they don't receive top marks in an exam, for example, then they have failed. Global statements about themselves and their behaviours are highly unlikely to be always true.

Scanning and hyper-vigilance

Clients may draw attention to themselves by scanning and being hyper-vigilant whilst out. When anxious it is common for us to become more sensitive to things happening in our environment. We look around checking to see that no-one is following or watching us. If we feel under threat this makes sense; we need reassurance that the environment is safe, that no-one is observing us, and that people are minding their own business. The trouble is that clients can draw attention to themselves by constantly looking over their shoulder. Their glances at other people make it more likely that others will notice them and look at them. When they do this, it only serves to raise their anxiety as they believe that "everyone" is staring at them. Instead clients could say to themselves, "I'm okay, I'm safe." "People are too busy shopping to be bothered with what I'm doing." By refocusing on the task of choosing groceries they are less likely to draw attention to themselves and less likely to be noticed.

Negative automatic thoughts

One or more of the identities may have negative automatic thoughts. Hence, for example, if an elderly lady smiles at them, they may automatically assume that this is for some negative reason, rather than seeing it for what it is, a smile. They cannot know for sure why the woman smiled and therefore would feel better if they could discount the negative thought and take the smile at face value. Negative thoughts haunt us all from time to time but their constant put downs do little for their self-esteem. I encourage clients to pay attention to the things they say to themselves and get them to challenge the negative thoughts which pop into their head. I ask them how true they are likely to be and suggest they go on a fact-finding mission looking at what evidence supports and refutes these beliefs. As mentioned previously, these clients often also have an internal persecutor who puts them down. I have discussed ways of working with persecutory alters previously. Suffice to say, this work is different in that these persecutory remarks should be worked through with host and alter together (for more details see under persecutory alters and challenging faulty beliefs).

Ignoring the positive

When clients complete tasks and successfully manage their anxiety, they have coped. I encourage clients to remember this, since it can be all too easy for them to ignore the times when things go well. By remembering these incidents clients can challenge their negative thinking that everything always goes wrong.

Rehearsing anxiety-provoking situations

Before embarking on something which is likely to be anxiety-provoking, I sometimes encourage clients to rehearse succeeding beforehand. I get them to go through the whole event in detail in their mind, image by image, word for word. By doing this, I let them see and hear themselves succeed before they do it for real.

* * *

Summary

Therapy with clients with DID will differ in structure and content.

Structural differences

- Therapy tends to be long term.
- Sessions are usually more frequent, sometimes two to three per week.
- Sessions may be one and a half hours during the middle phase of therapy.
- Extra work may be necessary between sessions.

Content differences

- One therapy approach is unlikely to be sufficient.
- A knowledge and use of a variety of techniques is helpful to inform treatment.
- Treatment may differ in the following ways:
  1. The therapist needs to manage the pace and timing of disclosure, as self-disclosure without permission can result in self-harming incidents, or suicide attempts.
  2. Therapy often involves psycho-education:
     a. Where the client learns to manage her feelings better, reducing the likelihood of her becoming overwhelmed or needing to resort to dissociation, or harmful behaviours.
     b. Psycho-education about dissociation and multiplicity is necessary as therapy aims to foster cooperation, communication, and collaboration among the identities.
  3. Therapy can resemble family therapy, where all identities need to be heard.

Techniques and strategies include:

1. **Motivational interviewing:**
   a. Looking at the advantages and disadvantages of a behaviour.
   b. Motivational interviewing may unearth information about a client's unhelpful behaviours.
   c. Understanding behaviours is the first step to tackling them.

2. **Breathing and relaxation exercises** can be taught to help the client manage anxiety.
3. **Graded exposure** can be used to encourage the client to take on new tasks.
4. **Distraction activities** help clients to focus on something other than their anxiety. I use one of two basic types of distraction: thought or behavioural distractions.
5. **Coping statements** are useful to encourage clients to challenge their anxiety.
6. **Teaching clients about anxiety**, about the symptoms and how to manage them.
7. **Cognitive behaviour therapy** can be used to encourage clients to challenge their anxiety. We rehearse anxiety-provoking situations, and specific topics I cover include: avoidance, fortune-telling, catastrophising, black and white thinking and exaggeration, scanning and hyper-vigilance, negative automatic thoughts, and ignoring the positive.

CHAPTER SEVEN

Problems and issues

Working with multiple selves

Working with clients with DID is likely to be more stressful for the practitioner, than working with clients who see themselves as individuals because the former are multiple. The therapist is not working with one but many identities and this factor on its own makes therapy harder to manage. However, given that one identity may not be aware that there are other identities, or of what another identity is doing, this makes therapy confusing to client and therapist alike. As mentioned previously it can make for a fine juggling act trying to take each identity into account when issues are discussed, particularly when it is evident that two or more identities hold contrasting positions.

In addition, a respondent in my research mentioned that therapy can be like backstitch in so far as an identity may talk about an event or issue and then forget the incident for a while. This may result in the account needing to be told on several occasions, sometimes by different identities and who may give slightly different accounts. Progress can thus feel frustratingly slow, particularly where issues have been addressed with one alter but remain problematic for another. At these times it can feel like therapy has reached stalemate, as similar issues come back around again in a very similar form. This can be hard to manage when the relationship is long term and at a minimum of once a week, often twice.

Difficulties working with the alters

There are frequently young alters who are demanding of attention. Coping with incessant demands can be draining and difficult to manage. I have had two reports from therapists who have had an identity turn up unannounced outside the therapist's home, or workplace, wanting to be seen. Also identities have telephoned or sent text messages incessantly. This has led to some therapists ending the therapy relationship, which is particularly damaging for this client group as usually they have experienced a succession of disrupted attachment relationships in their past.

Whilst some alters may want to cling and present as needy, others may be aggressive and hostile and may attempt to sabotage therapy. This can test the therapist to the limits making for challenging work. For example, I had one alter who was about ten years old attend a couple of sessions. Each time I attempted to call the host back to session he would prevent her by saying he would "get her later". This usually meant he would keep the host awake all night. Also he would shout at the other identities, upset or annoy them, causing the young ones to be scared and the older ones to be irritated, which left the host feeling exhausted. On one occasion when the alter arrived to session I asked if I could speak to the host. "Dunno" was the reply. After repeated failed attempts to raise the host, the conversation went along the lines of, "As I cannot speak to (the host) perhaps we can talk instead." "Dunno." "I am wondering why you are here because you don't seem to want to talk to me but you also seem to be stopping others talking too." "So?" "Well I am wondering why that is?" "Dunno" coupled with a smile as he thinks he is beginning to irritate me. He taps his foot and sighs. I begin to talk about why I think he is behaving this way. He feigns boredom by sighing and looking at his watch. "You don't want me to speak to (host) and you don't seem to want to talk and when I talk you look bored. What are we to do?" "Dunno." Whilst it took only two sessions to work through this alter's issue with therapy, I felt completely exhausted after these sessions. He had become very adept at working out how to keep his distance from people and I think it would work a treat with many!

Risk issues

Occasionally I have had experience of a host disappearing for a few days leaving a vulnerable child identity who has very limited ego strength to cope alone. This issue raises the point about the risk that the client poses to herself and how the therapist manages this. I have had debates as to whether the client has sufficient ego strength to keep herself safe and out of danger at these times. Who is responsible on these occasions? For example, I would have cause for concern about the safety of a child alter if she were to keep returning to a relative who abused her. Fortunately, when I have come across these sorts of problems, I have had the support of one of the client's friends or relatives who has stepped in for a while and ensured that the client stays safe.

Aside from the risk that clients may pose to themselves, some pose a risk to other people. Moskowitz (2004) wrote: "It is concluded that dissociation predicts violence in a wide range of populations and may be crucial to an understanding of violent behavior" (p. 21).

Also:

> According to Tanay, a forensic psychiatrist, 70% of the 53 homicide offenders, who were evaluated by him over a 10-year period, had been in a dissociative reaction when they committed the crime.

> (Moskowitz, 2004, p. 25)

Most studies cite dissociation as a major component in violent and criminal behaviours (Mazur, 2011). Where an identity fears for her own safety, this can result in assault, or attempted murder as the identity "defends" against what she sees as a perpetrator (Ringrose, 2010). To my knowledge, in my private practice, I have not had direct experience of working with a client with DID who has assaulted or murdered someone. However, I met several cases of in-patients with DID who had committed offences, whilst I was working in forensic services. I have also heard of a couple of clients who caused physical harm to professionals who had been restraining them in order to provide medical treatment, or who had tried to prevent the client from running away. These clients were seen by psychotherapists working in private practice. Hence, occasionally where clients become fearful, they may lash out at those trying to help them.

In addition, the client poses a high risk to herself in respect to cutting, self harming, and attempting suicide (Tatarelli et al. 2007). Hence, practitioners who do not like working with clients who harm themselves will need to give this client group a wide berth. Psychotherapists choosing to work with these clients may find managing the clients' risk to themselves difficult. Specifically, it can be hard striking the right balance of contact when the client has a crisis. On the one hand, the client needs to know she can turn to the therapist during difficult times but, on the other hand, the therapist must not inadvertently teach the client that she needs to have a crisis in order to get her needs met. Similarly, the client needs to learn to respect the boundaries between client and therapist; this is an area which these clients usually find difficult.

Problems encountered when the client is still experiencing abuse

Many clients with DID may still be being abused when they embark on therapy, or the abuse may have stopped but there is still contact or the threat of contact with an abuser in the client's current life. Sometimes clients' claims of current abuse may be the result of them being confused over what is current and what has happened in their past. However, where the abuse is still occurring, some practitioners argue it is advisable for the client to continue to be able to dissociate because she is likely to need that capacity in order to be able to manage. In these circumstances, the client needs to be able to maintain the ability to dissociate but at the same time work needs to explore the inner landscape of the client in such a way that a realistic chance of stopping ongoing abuse can be achieved. Balancing out both necessities at the same time is incredibly difficult for the therapist to manage. For a subgroup of these clients, who are involved with multiple abusers or organized criminality, it may take years for the client to separate herself from these harmful people. In the meantime, for some cases this can be dangerous work for client and therapist alike.

Somatoform symptoms can hamper treatment

Clients may come to therapy with multiple physical complaints that they attribute to physical disease. Often there has been a succession of doctors looking into these symptoms with limited success. However, despite there being little or no evidence of a physical complaint, clients will find it much easier to absolve responsibility for their symptoms and hand over their complaint to doctors to find solutions. Whilst this is understandable, in these cases work may be protracted and difficult as clients are invited to explore the possibility that these physical ailments are manifestations of psychological trauma.

Disadvantages to losing the ability to dissociate

There are many downsides to the client with DID losing their ability to dissociate and split off parts of herself. A common problem is the client's inability to tolerate conflicting emotions. Often different feelings are held with different identities and thus identities are not used to feeling ambivalent.

I have also found that the host can find it hard to accept parts of herself that she could before attribute to one of her alters. A typical feeling which is held in an alter is anger and as this tends to have been poorly controlled by the alter, it has usually caused the host problems. The consequence of this is that she has learnt that anger is a bad emotion that must always be suppressed, ignored, or passed off as uncontrollable because it belongs to an alter.

However, my favourite example of both the downside and upside of losing the ability to dissociate came from one of my research participants. She told me that one of her clients said on arrival in therapy: "Okay, you're on my shit list." The client was on crutches and her leg was in plaster. The therapist said: "Okay, what did I do now?" To which the client replied: "I was on the swing and I had my leg tucked under me and the swing broke and I fell and broke my leg and I felt it!" The therapist celebrated the event because ordinarily the client would have dissociated and would not have felt the pain (Ringrose, 2010).

Therapists and clients often receive limited support

Unfortunately, with all the difficulties and challenges that arise from working with these clients and when practitioners arguably need more support, this help is likely to be difficult to find and will need to be carefully selected. In the UK, specialist practitioners in this field are rare and thinly dispersed across the country. Also in society as a whole, there is still a lack of understanding, or an unwillingness to accept that psychological trauma is related to mental ill health. Unfortunately the medical profession's reliance on medication to treat all mental ill health may serve to strengthen this belief, as pills are prescribed to treat trauma. Whilst psychotropic treatments can be extremely beneficial for some mental health conditions, in the treatment of DID there has been no known treatment that offers anything more than palliative support to help manage symptoms of depression, anxiety, impulsivity, and substance abuse (Simeon, 2006). Whilst in some cases this support is invaluable, in the UK too many clients seem to end up reliant on medication long term because this form of treatment is more accessible than psychotherapy. Part of the reason for this is because therapy practitioners are often not part of the community psychiatric team and are not accessed through the NHS, presumably because they are not viewed as cost effective.This short-sighted view fails to take into account the money psychotherapy can save the health service in terms of reduced A & E admissions (typically these clients repeatedly present for suturing and treatment and/or observation following an overdose) as well as the cost of keeping patients on medications long term. There are also welfare costs incurred because left untreated these clients are unlikely to be able to work. However, more pertinent to this discussion, dissociation is a form of avoidance, avoidance of the pain of trauma. Whilst this is understandable, these clients do not improve by avoiding and drugs can encourage an avoidance of facing problems by holding feelings in abeyance.

Dealing with the sceptics

In the UK, there are many practitioners and lay people alike who doubt the existence of DID. Why this concept seems to have attracted so much controversy is somewhat of a mystery given that it is like any other psychological concept in that it has been derived from decades of research. Today, DID is listed in DSM-IV-TR and also in the International Statistical Classification of Diseases & Related Health, Tenth Version (ICD-10) as Multiple Personality Disorder. The Dissociative Experiences Scale was devised as a means of testing the likelihood of clients having a dissociative disorder (Carlson & Putnam, 1986). It is the most widely used screening instrument for the dissociative disorders (Simeon & Abugel, 2006) and has been extensively researched and found to be internally consistent, reliable over time, and has good convergent and discriminant validity (Carlson et al., 1993). There is also the Structured Clinical Interview for DSM-IV Dissociative Disorders, the SCID-D (Steinberg et al., 1993) and the revised version (SCID-D-R) (Steinberg, 1994) developed for the assessment and diagnosis of a dissociative disorder. This latter instrument has been translated into several languages (indicative that researchers and practitioners in several countries want to use it) and has been found to have good-to-excellent inter-rater reliability and discriminant validity for diagnosing the five dissociative disorders (Draijer & Boon, 1993). The Somatoform Dissociation Questionnaire (SDQ-20), Nijenhuis et al. (1996) which measures somatoform symptoms commonly found in DID, has similarly been reported to have excellent internal consistency and construct validity (Nijenhuis, 2003). There are, therefore, a significant number of researchers and practitioners on both sides of the Atlantic and across Europe and Asia who have consistently and repeatedly identified the same clinical features over a period of decades. If DID does not exist as a viable construct there are a significant number of people wasting a great deal of time. I end this point with a quote from one of the respondents from my most recent study:

> To me the construct of DID is either useful or it is not—and that is a totally empirical question. The question is not "Do you believe DID exists, or does DID really exist?" DID is comprised of a set of observable behaviours and if a group of professionals can recognise these behaviours, agree that these behaviours are occurring, and agree that this constellation of behaviours indicates that we use certain intervention approaches, that's all we need. The DID construct then becomes a useful way of categorising behaviours.
>
> (Ringrose, 2011, p. 156)

Practitioners' challenges of the existence of DID have had consequences for its treatment. Practitioners can become more isolated as they are concerned about sharing their diagnosis with other professionals for fear of being ridiculed (Ringrose, 2010).

In addition, in my area of the UK, Yorkshire, in cases where many psychotherapists would prefer to work within a multidisciplinary team, where they can be better supported and where clients may benefit from additional support from other care workers as well as drug treatments, this will frequently not be forthcoming. Clients' psychotropic medication will often be prescribed and managed by the client's GP rather than the community psychiatrist and all too often the client has no further support than emergency out of hours services, or the accident and emergency department.

Where a community psychiatrist is involved, the care may be uncoordinated and performed in isolation from the therapy work. This is because sometimes where the therapist notifies the psychiatrist of the therapist's involvement, this will result in the removal of the client's community psychiatric nurse. This can mean that psychotherapists are left grossly unsupported and often only supported by their standard supervisor who is likely to have little understanding of DID.

As an aside, I have often had to phrase my account of the client's problems as complex trauma but not mention DID in order that practitioners will be able to digest it. On occasions if I said someone has DID the diagnosis would be dismissed. I am not alone in this practice. I am aware that by not identifying DID I am contributing to its "rarity". However, I tend to focus my energies on educating those I feel are most open to the possibility and hope that those who at the moment are not, will eventually be carried along by the remainder of us.

Vicarious and secondary trauma

The risk of vicarious trauma is one of the hazards of being a psychotherapist. However, for the therapist working with clients with DID this risk is arguably higher because of the severity of the trauma and the longevity of the therapy relationship. As is the case in working with clients with many other psychological problems, hearing the trauma experiences of clients may cause secondary trauma in the therapist, sometimes called compassion fatigue (Figley, 1986) or vicarious traumatisation (Pearlman & Saakvitne, 1995). However, arguably what heightens this problem is practitioner's fears of traumatising other therapists by talking about the trauma incidents of clients in supervision. This can mean that therapists keep a lot more of their experiences in therapy with this client group to themselves than they normally would. It will come as no surprise to read that there is a high level of burnout from working with this client group.

In the box below, I list some of the problems my research participants voiced in the course of their work with this client group.

Practitioners' comments on the problems of working with DID

"Sometimes some of the stuff is so sad and painful ... to hear ... not only I think it doesn't help the client but there is only so much I can tolerate without being too affected by it."

"When she talked, I was in shock or grief; it was about sexual assault."

"I have a long-term chronic illness and I think part of that is secondary trauma from working with clients."

"Someone literally self harming in front of you, that cannot be digested."

"He did this quite horrendous thing. I don't often talk about this because I may have traumatised people when I have explained this case in other forums."

"A lot of the work that we were doing was basic risk assessment, I would say keeping her alive, lots of suicide tendencies, eating disorder problems, self harm."

The "client had a very child-like alter who felt very vulnerable but he also had a very violent predatory alter, who was very capable of killing and would do so in response to the child-like alter feeling very vulnerable".

(Ringrose, 2010)

Limiting the risk of compassion fatigue and burnout

It is therefore imperative that practitioners take special care of themselves. Factors which help practitioners in this respect include:

1. Limiting the number of clients the practitioner works with who have DID.
2. Ensuring the practitioner's work with these clients is not the only work undertaken.
3. Having a lot of support from other practitioners who understand DID and have a degree of knowledge of the specific problems these clients bring and the difficulties these raise in the practitioner.
4. Undertaking a thorough risk assessment to ensure that the therapist can manage the client in the environment where he or she is working.

5. Compiling a strong contract with the client which covers several eventualities.
6. Having the option of a stand-in therapist who can take over clients whilst the main therapist is away.

I want to end with some of the rewards from working with clients with a diagnosis of DID. Despite all of the problems these clients bring, the advantages for me have far outweighed the disadvantages. The main benefit is the degree of change that is possible with this client group. This is not only great for clients but I get to freeload on the high which comes with it too. From the depths these clients have reached, like the proverbial saying goes, the only way is up, or I suppose there could be more of the same but this has not been my experience. I am in awe when I think about how these clients (usually as tiny children) have intuitively found ways to cope with the appalling experiences they have faced and how they have survived relatively intact. The power of the mind to find a solution like dissociation in order for the host to cope with the atrocities of life and keep going, is a wonder that I marvel at. How clever are the minds of these clients? Although their dissociative experiences may be causing problems for them now, I am pleased they found this way to cope because, without it, I wonder whether they would have survived.

* * *

Summary

Working with clients with DID presents many additional problems to those found in standard individual therapy.

- Clients with DID are multiple and need to be treated as such.
- Multiplicity presents difficulties when one or more alter personalities do not want to attend therapy.
- Practitioners are likely to need to think more carefully about managing the risk clients pose to themselves and others both in the therapy session and outside.
- Clients attending therapy who continue to experience abuse will need to retain the ability to dissociate but at the same time work towards ending the abusive relationship. Balancing these necessities at the same time is difficult to manage.
- Clients who experience somatoform symptoms may require longer in therapy because they may attribute these to physical disease and need time to realise otherwise.
- Clients experience disadvantages to losing the ability to dissociate, for example, experiencing ambivalence and physical pain which they may not have previously felt.
- Practitioner and client support is limited; specialist practitioners in this field are rare and widely dispersed.
- Practitioners' scepticism of DID has compounded the problem leaving therapists isolated.
- The medical profession's reliance on medication to treat trauma may encourage clients to avoid their issues by taking psychotropic drugs to keep feelings in abeyance.
- The risk of vicarious trauma is high due to the type and level of trauma experienced by these clients. Practitioners attempt to minimise this risk in several ways, for example by limiting the number of clients they see.

RESOURCES

Dissociative Experiences Scale (DES)
(Carlson & Putnam, 1986)

Directions: This questionnaire consists of twenty-eight questions about experiences that you may have in your daily life. We are interested in how often you have these experiences. It is important, however, that your answers show how often these experiences happen to you when you are not under the influence of alcohol or drugs. To answer the questions, please determine to what degree the experience described in the question applies to you and circle the number to show what percentage of the time you have the experience.

1. **Some people have the experience of driving a car and suddenly realising that they don't remember what has happened during all or part of the trip.**
   Circle a number to show what percentage of the time this happens to you.
   (never) 0% 10 20 30 40 50 60 70 80 90 100% (always)

2. **Some people find that sometimes they are listening to someone talk and they suddenly realise that they did not hear all or part of what was said.**
Circle a number to show what percentage of the time this happens to you.
(never) 0% 10 20 30 40 50 60 70 80 90 100% (always)

3. **Some people have the experience of finding themselves in a place and having no idea how they got there.**
Circle a number to show what percentage of the time this happens to you.
(never) 0% 10 20 30 40 50 60 70 80 90 100% (always)

4. **Some people have the experience of finding themselves dressed in clothes that they don't remember putting on.**
Circle a number to show what percentage of the time this happens to you.
(never) 0% 10 20 30 40 50 60 70 80 90 100% (always)

5. **Some people have the experience of finding new things among their belongings that they do not remember buying.**
Circle a number to show what percentage of the time this happens to you.
(never) 0% 10 20 30 40 50 60 70 80 90 100% (always)

6. **Some people sometimes find that they are approached by people that they do not know who call them by another name or insist that they have met them before.**
Circle a number to show what percentage of the time this happens to you.
(never) 0% 10 20 30 40 50 60 70 80 90 100% (always)

7. **Some people sometimes have the experience of feeling as though they are standing next to themselves or watching themselves do something as if they were looking at another person.**
Circle a number to show what percentage of the time this happens to you.
(never) 0% 10 20 30 40 50 60 70 80 90 100% (always)

8. **Some people are told that they sometimes do not recognise friends or family members.**
Circle a number to show what percentage of the time this happens to you.
(never) 0% 10 20 30 40 50 60 70 80 90 100% (always)

9. **Some people find that they have no memory for some important events in their lives (for example, a wedding or graduation).**
Circle a number to show what percentage of the time this happens to you.
(never) 0% 10 20 30 40 50 60 70 80 90 100% (always)

10. **Some people have the experience of being accused of lying when they do not think that they have lied.**
Circle a number to show what percentage of the time this happens to you.
(never) 0% 10 20 30 40 50 60 70 80 90 100% (always)

11. **Some people have the experience of looking in a mirror and not recognising themselves.**
Circle a number to show what percentage of the time this happens to you.
(never) 0% 10 20 30 40 50 60 70 80 90 100% (always)

12. **Some people sometimes have the experience of feeling that other people, objects, and the world around them are not real.**
Circle a number to show what percentage of the time this happens to you.
(never) 0% 10 20 30 40 50 60 70 80 90 100% (always)

13. **Some people sometimes have the experience of feeling that their body does not belong to them.**
Circle a number to show what percentage of the time this happens to you.
(never) 0% 10 20 30 40 50 60 70 80 90 100% (always)

14. **Some people have the experience of sometimes remembering a past event so vividly that they feel as if they were reliving that event.**

Circle a number to show what percentage of the time this happens to you.
(never) 0% 10 20 30 40 50 60 70 80 90 100% (always)

15. **Some people have the experience of not being sure whether things that they remember happening really did happen or whether they just dreamed them.**
Circle a number to show what percentage of the time this happens to you.
(never) 0% 10 20 30 40 50 60 70 80 90 100% (always)

16. **Some people have the experience of being in a familiar place but finding it strange and unfamiliar.**
Circle a number to show what percentage of the time this happens to you.
(never) 0% 10 20 30 40 50 60 70 80 90 100% (always)

17. **Some people find that when they are watching television or a movie they become so absorbed in the story that they are unaware of other events happening around them.**
Circle a number to show what percentage of the time this happens to you.
(never) 0% 10 20 30 40 50 60 70 80 90 100% (always)

18. **Some people sometimes find that they become so involved in a fantasy or daydream that it feels as though it were really happening to them.**
Circle a number to show what percentage of the time this happens to you.
(never) 0% 10 20 30 40 50 60 70 80 90 100% (always)

19. **Some people find that they are sometimes able to ignore pain.**
Circle a number to show what percentage of the time this happens to you.
(never) 0% 10 20 30 40 50 60 70 80 90 100% (always)

20. **Some people find that they sometimes sit staring off into space, thinking of nothing, and are not aware of the passage of time.**

Circle a number to show what percentage of the time this happens to you.

(never) 0% 10 20 30 40 50 60 70 80 90 100% (always)

21. **Some people sometimes find that when they are alone they talk out loud to themselves.**
Circle a number to show what percentage of the time this happens to you.
(never) 0% 10 20 30 40 50 60 70 80 90 100% (always)

22. **Some people find that in one situation they may act so differently compared with another that they feel almost as if they were different people.**
Circle a number to show what percentage of the time this happens to you.
(never) 0% 10 20 30 40 50 60 70 80 90 100% (always)

23. **Some people sometimes find that in certain situations they are able to do things with amazing ease and spontaneity that would usually be difficult for them (for example, sports, work, social situations, etc.).**
Circle a number to show what percentage of the time this happens to you.
(never) 0% 10 20 30 40 50 60 70 80 90 100% (always)

24. **Some people sometimes find that they cannot remember whether they have done something or have just thought about doing that thing (for example, not knowing whether they have just mailed a letter or have just thought about mailing it).**
Circle a number to show what percentage of the time this happens to you.
(never) 0% 10 20 30 40 50 60 70 80 90 100% (always)

25. **Some people find evidence that they have done things that they do not remember doing.**
Circle a number to show what percentage of the time this happens to you.
(never) 0% 10 20 30 40 50 60 70 80 90 100% (always)

26. **Some people sometimes find writings, drawings, or notes among their belongings that they must have done but cannot remember doing.**
Circle a number to show what percentage of the time this happens to you.
(never) 0% 10 20 30 40 50 60 70 80 90 100% (always)

27. **Some people find that they sometimes hear voices inside their head that tell them to do things or comment on things that they are doing.**
Circle a number to show what percentage of the time this happens to you.
(never) 0% 10 20 30 40 50 60 70 80 90 100% (always)

28. **Some people sometimes feel as if they are looking at the world through a fog so that people or objects appear far away or unclear.**
Circle a number to show what percentage of the time this happens to you.
(never) 0% 10 20 30 40 50 60 70 80 90 100% (always)

Somatoform Dissociation Questionnaire (SDQ – 20)
(Nijenhuis et al., 1996)

This questionnaire asks about different physical symptoms or body experiences, which you may have had either briefly or for a longer time. Please indicate to what extent these experiences apply to you **in the past year**. For each statement, please circle the number in the first column that best applies to YOU.

The possibilities are:

1 = this applies to me NOT AT ALL
2 = this applies to me A LITTLE
3 = this applies to me MODERATELY
4 = this applies to me QUITE A BIT
5 = this applies to me EXTREMELY.

If a symptom or experience applies to you, please indicate whether a **physician** has connected it with a **physical disease**. Indicate this by circling the word YES or NO in the column: "Is the physical cause known?" If you wrote YES, please write the physical cause (if you know it) on the line.

Example:

Extent to which the symptom or experience applies to you	Is the physical cause cause known?

Sometimes:

my teeth chatter 1 2 3 4 5	NO	YES, namely ....
I have cramps in my calves 1 2 3 4 5	NO	YES, namely ....

If you have circled a 1 in the first column (i.e., This applies to me NOT AT ALL), you do NOT have to respond to the question about whether the physical cause is known.

On the other hand, if you circle 2, 3, 4, or 5, you MUST circle No or YES in the "Is the physical cause known?" column.

Please do not skip any of the 20 questions.

Thank you for your cooperation.

Here are the questions:

1 = this applies to me NOT AT ALL
2 = this applies to me A LITTLE
3 = this applies to me MODERATELY
4 = this applies to me QUITE A BIT
5 = this applies to me EXTREMELY.

	Extent to which the symptom or experience applies to you	Is the physical cause known?		
Sometimes:				
1. I have trouble urinating	1 2 3 4 5	No	Yes,	namely
2. I dislike tastes that I usually like (women: at times OTHER THAN pregnancy or monthly periods)	1 2 3 4 5	No	Yes,	namely
3. I hear sounds from nearby as if they were coming from far away	1 2 3 4 5	No	Yes,	namely
4. I have pain while urinating	1 2 3 4 5	No	Yes,	namely
5. My body, or a part of it, feels numb	1 2 3 4 5	No	Yes,	namely
6. People and things look bigger than usual	1 2 3 4 5	No	Yes,	namely
7. I have an attack that resembles an epileptic seizure	1 2 3 4 5	No	Yes,	namely
8. My body, or a part of it, is insensitive to pain	1 2 3 4 5	No	Yes,	namely

9. I dislike smells that I
usually like   1 2 3 4 5   No   Yes,   namely
....

10. I feel pain in my genitals
(at times OTHER THAN
sexual intercourse)   1 2 3 4 5   No   Yes,   namely
....

11. I cannot hear for a while
(as if I am deaf)   1 2 3 4 5   No   Yes,   namely
....

12. I cannot see for a while
(as if I am blind)   1 2 3 4 5   No   Yes,   namely
....

13. I see things around me
differently than usual (for
example, as if looking through
a tunnel, or seeing merely a
part of an object)   1 2 3 4 5   No   Yes,   namely
....

14. I am able to smell much
BETTER or WORSE than
I usually do (even though
I do not have a cold)   1 2 3 4 5   No   Yes,   namely
....

15. It is as if my body, or a part
of it, has disappeared   1 2 3 4 5   No   Yes,   namely
....

16. I cannot swallow, or can swallow
only with great effort   1 2 3 4 5   No   Yes,   namely
....

17. I cannot sleep for nights on end,
but remain very active during
daytime   1 2 3 4 5   No   Yes,   namely
....

18. I cannot speak (or only
with great effort) or I
can only whisper   1 2 3 4 5   No   Yes,   namely
....

19. I am paralysed for
    a while   1 2 3 4 5   No   Yes,   namely
    ....
20. I grow stiff for a while   1 2 3 4 5   No   Yes,   namely
    ....

Before continuing, will you please check whether you have responded to all twenty statements?
You are asked to fill in and place an X beside what applies to you.

21. Age: .... years
22. Sex: .... female .... male
23. Marital status: .... single .... married .... living together ....
    divorced .... widower/widow
24. Education: .... number of years
25. Date: ....
26. Name: ....

Organizations for practitioners, clients, and their families

Trauma and Abuse Group (TAG)	
PO Box 3295	A group run for professionals and carers alike. Providing information support and training.
SWINDON	
SN2 9ED	
www.tag-uk.net	
membershipsec@tag-uk.net	

First Person Plural	
PO Box 2537	A registered charity run by people with experience of dissociation and who have survived abuse. Open to professionals, survivors, and carers wanting information and support.
WOLVERHAMPTON	
WV4 4ZL	
www.firstpersonplural.org.uk	
fpp@firstpersonplural.org.uk	

PODS (Partners of Dissociative Survivors)	
PO Box 633	Open to the partners of people with dissociative experiences. Offering information and practical support on how to care for people with dissociative experiences and their families.
HUNTINGDON	
Cambridgeshire	
PE29 9GJ	
www.tasc-online.org.uk/pods	

Ritual Abuse Information Network & Support (RAINS)	
PO Box 458	A support group aimed at survivors of ritual satanic abuse.
Godalming	
Surrey	
GU7 2YT	
01483 898600	

European Society for the Study of Trauma & Dissociation	
1ste Hogeweg 16-a	An organisation promoting all aspects pertaining to the field of dissociation. Promoting research and training in the field, as well as providing information on the dissociative disorders to interested parties.
3701 HK Zeist	
The Netherlands	
0031 30 6977841	
info@estd.org	
www.estd.org	

International Society for the Study of Trauma & Dissociation	
8400 Westpark Drive	Promotes research, training, knowledge of trauma and dissociation, and supports communication amongst clinicians working in the field.
Second Floor	
McLean VA 22102	
www.isst-d.org	
info@isst-d.org	

Managing anxiety

Progressive relaxation exercise

The following exercise was devised by Edmund Jacobson (cited in Bernstein & Borkovec, 1973). For each of the following body parts tense the muscle (without straining) concentrate on the feeling of tension, hold for five seconds and then relax for ten seconds. Pay attention to how the muscles feel when they are relaxed and breathe slowly and regularly throughout the exercises.

- **Feet:** Sit with your legs outstretched, point your toes and curl them back, tense the muscles in your feet, repeat and relax.
- **Legs:** Straighten your legs, point your toes towards your face, and feel the tension in the back of your carves. Relax, let your legs go limp and repeat.
- **Stomach:** Tense your stomach muscles by pulling them in and up, as if preparing to be punched. Relax and repeat.
- **Back:** Arch your back, feel the tension in the base of your spine. Relax and repeat.
- **Shoulders and Neck:** Shrug your shoulders as hard as you can, bringing them up towards your ears and in. Press your head back. Relax and repeat.
- **Arms:** Stretch your arms out straight and clench your fists. Relax and let your arms hang limp and repeat.
- **Face:** Tense your forehead and jaw. Lower your eyebrows and bite hard. Relax and repeat.
- **Whole Body:** Tense your entire body, your feet, legs, stomach, back, shoulders, neck, arms, and face. Hold the tension for a few seconds. Relax and repeat.

The routine can be repeated if you still feel tense. If only parts of you feel tense, repeat for those parts. Take some time to relax your mind. Conjure up an image or scene which you find peaceful, perhaps a favourite garden, river, or somewhere at the seaside. Imagine seeing, hearing, and smelling or tasting things that remind you of the scene. Breathe slowly and deeply for a few minutes.

Breathing techniques

Breathing and tensing muscles to aid relaxation (Owen, 2005)

Breathing exercises are useful techniques to try when feeling anxious because they can be done virtually anywhere and for some people, can quickly bring a sense of calm. They need to be started at the first sign of anxiety, or tension. The following exercise can be done without other people knowing.

1. Breathe in slowly and deeply, counting six to eight seconds to do this. At the same time, slowly clench your fists.
2. Hold your breath with fists clenched counting for four seconds and focus on the feeling of tension in your fists.
3. Slowly breathe out and let your fists unclench over a period of about eight seconds.
4. Focus on the relief from tension and say in your head a long drawn out "relax" as the tension is released, and, breathing out, allow your body to become relaxed and loose.
5. Repeat the technique as necessary.

Breathing during a panic attack

During a panic attack people tend to breathe very fast, which reduces the amount of carbon dioxide in the lungs, creating unpleasant body sensations (for example, tingling in the hands and feeling dizzy). To stop this from happening, or to restore calm, the amount of carbon dioxide needs to be raised.

This can be achieved by placing a PAPER bag (never plastic) over your mouth and nose and breathing in and out until you feel yourself calm down. If you don't happen to have a paper bag to hand, this can still be accomplished with sufficient success to bring relief, by cupping your hands over your nose and mouth and breathing gently for two to three minutes until calm is restored.

Alternatively, simply by breathing in and out slowly, evenly and deeply, balance can be restored. It is sometimes easier to count one thousand elephants (any three-syllable word will do!) slowly to yourself as you breathe in and two thousand elephants as you breathe out. Try to ensure you breathe all the way out. Like this:

In	Out	In	Etc.
1,000 elephants	2,000 elephants	3,000 elephants	

Sometimes when people feel very panicked, remembering what to count and when can be too difficult and people end up muddled. You could talk to a friend about your difficulty when you are feeling calm. Ask your friend if he or she will help at these times by allowing you to put your hands on his or her shoulders. Ask your friend to exaggerate his or her breathing in and out slowly so that you can feel his or her shoulders move upwards and downwards. Copy your friend's breathing rate, and try to stay in time with him or her. Once your breathing has slowed, you need to return to a normal pattern, reverting to breathing "through" your tummy. See below under long-term practice.

Long-term practice

Over-breathing is a normal reaction to stress—where there is a natural increase in the rate and depth of breathing—but if allowed to continue you may develop the habit of over-breathing most of the time. The following technique is called the Papworth breathing technique and is specifically designed to be used in the treatment of over-breathing (Holloway, 2007).

Continuous over-breathing causes a lowering of carbon dioxide levels in the bloodstream, and because the blood circulates all around the body, it can cause many different symptoms. The most common ones are shortness of breath, tingling in the hands and feet, muscle tremors and cramps, headaches, dizziness, and indigestion. Treatment aims to correct your breathing pattern and help you relax.

Normal breathing pattern

Your normal breathing pattern should be gentle, silent diaphragmatic or tummy breathing with very little upper chest movement. The rate should be about eight to ten average size breaths a minute at rest.

Hyperventilation or over-breathing pattern

An over-breathing pattern is erratic and sometimes noisy; breathing is mainly from the upper chest. The rate of breathing is fast, often more than fifteen breaths a minute and the depth of each breath varies, sometimes giving deep sighs.

Breathing exercises

Become aware of your breathing by placing one hand on your upper chest and one on your tummy. Let your upper chest relax down and with the next breath allow your tummy to swell forward as you breathe in and fall back gently as you breathe out. Try to get a steady rhythm going taking the same depth of breath each time. Next try to slow your breathing rate down by putting in a short pause after you have breathed out and before you breathe in again. At first you may feel you are not getting enough air in but with regular practice this slower rate will soon feel comfortable.

Breathing is something you do all the time so check that you have got it right in all positions whether lying, sitting, or standing. When exercising there will be a natural increase in your breathing rate but check afterwards to make sure that you go back to a slow, steady rhythm. Try to talk slowly, do not say too much with one breath and pause to take gentle breaths in from your tummy before carrying on.

Tackling fears through graded exposure

Graded exposure will not be useful in all cases of DID and is unlikely to be useful in the beginning stage of treatment. This is because the host(s) needs to have sufficient adult ego strength to be able to separate herself from her child identities and sufficiently well for her to be able to expose herself to the feared situation but without a switch occurring whilst carrying out the task. In cases where a task is avoided, for example because the alter(s) fears the task (usually because it is reminiscent of past trauma) and the host picks up the alter's(s') fears but has no memory of the original trauma, the host can encourage alter(s) to go to a safe place whilst she manages the task. In these circumstances, fears can be tackled taking a two-pronged approach: the first involving the host's graded exposure to the task, and, then eventually, the second looking at the underlying source of the fear by working through the alter's(s') trauma.

Kennerley (1997) has written an excellent book for clients and practitioners that describes ways to manage anxiety. Fears can be overcome by using a technique called graded exposure, where clients are introduced to their feared situations in small manageable steps. Below I outline the main steps and key issues to consider at each stage.

Assessing the problem

Before tackling a problem there are a few things to look at first.

a. Decide on the fears to be tackled. Often there is more than one but some are likely to matter more than others. Make a list of the ones that have the greatest impact on daily living, or those that are the most important.

b. Put them into the sequence in which they are to be tackled. Sometimes the thing that is causing the most anxiety, is not the first thing to be faced because it may be necessary to begin with something less difficult.

c. Having decided which task to focus on first, set about finding out more about the nature of the fear. For the first fear to be tackled, ask a series of questions.

   • Does the size (of shop, spider, lift, group) make a difference?
   • Does the number of people involved make a difference?
   • Is there a better or worse time of day (e.g., busy *vs.* quiet)?
   • What makes it easier or harder to cope when doing the task?

Example

Jenny (host) has alter personalities who are afraid of small spaces because they were locked in the under stairs cupboard. This has meant that Jenny has found her work life increasingly stressful because she has found that she has to use the lift in the high-rise building where she works, several times a day. This reminds her young identities of abuse incidents and she goes into panic in response. As host, she has found it embarrassing at times because colleagues have commented on her not using the lift, or taking a long time over her tasks. She has also stopped going out with colleagues for lunch because she does not want them to see her scared in the lift and she does not want to have to explain why she always uses the stairs. Jenny can ask the alters who fear small spaces to go somewhere safe whilst she is at work. In addition Jenny's adult ego strength may be fostered by her managing the current situation through graded exposure. For Jenny this means using the questions above to examine what it is about the lift she does not like.

- Jenny believes that she would be better in larger lifts than smaller ones.
- She feels better when there is at least one other person going all the way with her but when the lift is not jam-packed.
- She finds it harder the longer she has to be in the lift, going only one or two floors would be easier.
- She does not like her colleagues to be in the lift with her because she fears they will notice she is scared and she then feels silly. This she fears will push her over the edge and cause her to retreat.
- She thinks she would find it easier to go in the lift when there are fewer people around and therefore not at clocking on or clocking off times.

Goal setting

Next Jenny needs to decide precisely what she wants to achieve in terms of conquering her fear. How would she know she had succeeded? It is important to be very specific when setting goals.

Jenny's goal

Jenny believes that she will have conquered her fear if she can ride in any lift, large or small, at any time of day (quiet or busy) either alone or with a group of people.

Facing fears in manageable steps

Next it is important to write down, in a series of stages from least to most feared, where to begin to tackle the fear by actively doing each task. When devising this list, it is important that each stage is sufficiently difficult to be a challenge, but it should be one that the host feels able to complete. It is important to build confidence slowly by succeeding at each stage along the way. Also ensure that tasks are feasible and practical. For example, it would be no good setting a target of doing a task with a close friend when the close friend may be unavailable.

Jenny's steps

Step 1: Jenny commits to riding in a large lift, at a quiet time, with a close colleague, up two floors once a day for a week.

Step 2: Jenny commits to repeat step 1, going up or down two floors, with her colleague but to increase this to two or three times a day for a week.

Step 3: Jenny commits to stay in the large lift all the way up to the top floor. She arranges to meet her colleague who will accompany her at the beginning and end of the day for this purpose. Jenny continues to ride in the lift up or down two floors with her colleague between.

Step 4: Jenny repeats step 3 for a week. She commits to do two shorter trips a day on her own.

Step 5: Jenny continues using the lift at work riding at the beginning and end of the day with her friend and on her own for shorter rides between. In addition, she begins to use different lifts to go up or down one or two floors with her friend whilst out shopping at quiet times.

Step 6: Jenny continues with step 5 but now she rides four floors at work on her own at lunchtime. She commits to do this everyday for a week.

Step 7: Jenny continues to travel in the lift according to her schedule at work. She also rides in small and large lifts whilst out shopping on a busier but not packed day.

Step 8: Jenny tackles using the lift at work on her own whenever she needs to. She also travels in small and large lifts whenever necessary whether it is quiet or busy.

Main points

Each step must feel achievable and not too much at once. Success is more important than speed as this may result in a step being unsuccessful.

Keep some pressure on when designing tasks and keep practising. The feared thing must be done regularly, otherwise it is harder to maintain.

Encourage the host to give themselves a pat on the back when each step is completed. Discourage the host from self criticism for failure to complete a task. Where tasks are not successfully completed this tends to be because the step was too high (like the rises of a staircase). A further step may need to be put in-between or a previous step may need to be repeated.

Keep repeating tasks until they can be completed without fear. If different situations influence the likelihood of completing a task, make sure the task is completed in all these situations and without feeling anxious. When this is achieved people tend to have overcome their fear and can begin with the next task on their list.

Problem-shooting

Think creatively when designing schedules, this is only one example. It may be that initially Jenny could not begin by going up two floors with her friend. In this case, she could have stood in the lift with her friend with the doors open. If lifts were too frightening it may be that initially she performed the task visually imagining each stage of travelling in a lift up one floor. Once she feels confident with this, then she could begin by standing in the lift without it moving.

Sometimes people need to try out a similar experience first. For example, Jenny found that it was being locked in a confined space that she disliked about travelling in the lift. She could therefore ask a friend to lock her in a small room for a short period of time.

Sometimes people become extremely anxious whilst facing their fears. This may be because:

- The task is too difficult a challenge and an additional step needs putting in-between.

- The host may need longer doing the previous step in order to build up confidence.
- Hosts may need to practise the feared event in their mind through imagery first. These can be practised alongside breathing exercises and relaxation techniques before "going live".
- Further reassurance may be necessary at the time of undertaking the task. Often people benefit from their therapist, or a friend accompanying them, as they can offer support in helping the host stay calm and assist them in regulating their breathing.

Techniques and strategies for coping with self-harm and overwhelming feelings

Clients with DID commonly have an alter who self harms because she is angry, frustrated, or sad. Alternatively, the host may self harm in order to encourage a switch or because she is suffering from depersonalisation symptoms such as feeling unreal, or numb and want to ground herself. The reason behind the self-harming is important information because different activities are better suited to relieve the urge to self-harm depending on the reason for the desire (Ringrose, 2010; Sirius, 2011). Also knowing which alter personality(ies) self harm is necessary in order for the host to work alongside the alter. Partaking in one or more of these activities may stave off the need to self-harm long enough for it to become unnecessary.

Anger, frustration, or agitation

Where anger, frustration, or agitation foster the desire to self-harm it may help to:

- Do something physical or energetic.
- Visit the bottle bank and smash bottles, or alternatively flatten cans for recycling.
- Tear up newspapers.
- Cut up a photograph or a picture.
- Throw ice, preferably outside, or in the bathroom but throw it hard enough to shatter.
- Listen to music on high volume and shout out the words. Some songs are better than others!
- Go for a brisk walk.

Sadness, depression, or unhappiness

If the feeling that is fostering the desire to self-harm is sadness, depression, or unhappiness:

- Quieter, stiller activities usually are the most effective.
- Partaking in hobbies like painting, fishing, or playing a musical instrument.

- Taking a soothing bath with bubbles and candles or incense.
- Watching a feel-good film.
- Walking in the countryside.
- Playing golf, or a game, which is less physical in nature like croquet or bowls.
- Listening to calming music or a relaxation CD, for example, one with water flowing and birds singing.
- Moisturising the body.
- Going to bed with a book and a warm drink.
- Phoning or visiting a friend.

Numb, unreal, detached, distant

If the feelings that are fostering the desire to self-harm centre around feeling numb, distant, detached, or unreal:

- Activities which create sharp intense sensations are the most effective.
- Chewing on something strongly flavoured, a garlic clove, a piece of root ginger, or a chilli.
- Slapping a hard surface.
- Taking a cold bath.
- Stamping feet heavily.
- Squeezing an ice cube. This can be placed in the area where the client wants to cut or burn him or herself as it leaves a red mark afterwards.
- Wearing an elastic band around the wrist which can be flexed when the client begins to feel as if he or she may dissociate. This can help to bring him or her back.

Wanting to see blood

In some cases clients feel they need to see blood. Activities which may help with this are:

- Drawing on the skin with a red felt-tip pen, or an ice cube coloured with red food colouring, where self-harming normally takes place.
- Squeezing ice cubes previously coloured with red dye.

Missing the habitual ritual of self-harming

Where clients miss the habitual nature of their self-harming ritual, it may help to:

- Visualise each step of the self-injury routine in the smallest detail. It may be helpful for you to bandage yourself afterwards as if you had self-harmed.
- Distract
  1. With thought tasks. For example, describe an everyday object to an alien.
  2. By doing something that gets you up and moving about. For example, gardening, tidying, or cleaning.
- Postpone carrying out the ritual for as long as possible because it may pass.

REFERENCES

Allison, R. B. (1978). A rational psychotherapy plan for multiplicity. In: F. W. Putnam (Ed.), *Diagnosis and Treatment of Multiple Personality Disorder* (*pp. 9–16*). London: The Guilford Press.

American Psychiatric Association (2000). *Diagnostic & Statistical Manual of Mental Disorders, Fourth Edition*, text revision. Washington, DC.

Aquarone, R. (2009). Audio-recorded interview for thesis entitled "Dissociative identity disorder and the dissociative disorders: an exploration of contemporary theory and practice" (unpublished doctoral thesis, Metanoia Institute, London, UK, 2010).

Arthur Rifkin, M. D., Dione Ghisalbert, D. O., Sonia Dimatou, M. D., Charles Jin, M. D. & Mohammed Sethi, M. D. (1998). Identity disorder in psychiatric inpatients. *American Journal of Psychiatry, 155*: 844–845.

Bernstein, D. A. & Borkovec, T. D. (1973). *Progressive Relaxation Training: A manual for the helping professions*. Champaign: IL Research Press.

Braun, B. G. (1988). The BASK model of dissociation: Alter II Treatment. *Dissociation, 1*(2): 16–23.

Briere, J. (1995). *Trauma Symptom Inventory Professional Manual*. Odessa, FL: Psychological Assessment Resources.

Cardeña, E. (1994). *Dissociation Clinical and Theoretical Perspectives*. Lynn, S. J. & Rhue, J. W. (Eds.). New York: Guilford Press.

119

120   REFERENCES

Cardeña, E. & Weiner, L. (2004). Evaluation of dissociation across the lifespan. *Psychotherapy, 41*: 496–508.

Carlson, E. & Putnam, F. W. (1986). Development reliability and validity of a dissociation scale. *Journal of Nervous and Mental Diseases, 174*(12): 727–735. (Updated April 2010) Available at: http://counsellingresource.com/quizzes/des/index.html [Accessed 28 March 2012].

Carlson, E. B. & Putnam, F. W. (1993). An update on the dissociative experiences scale. *Dissociation, 6*(4): 16–27.

Carlson, E. B., Putnam, F. W., Ross, C. A., Torem, M., Coons, P., Dill, D., Loewenstein, R. J. & Baum, B. G. (1993). Validity of the dissociative experiences scale in screening for MPD: A multi centre study. *American Journal of Psychiatry, 150*(7): 1,030–1,036.

Coons, P. M., Bowman, E. S. & Milstein, V. (1988). Multiple personality disorder. *Nervous & Mental Disease, 176*(9): 519–527.

Draijer, N. & Boon, S. (1993). The validation of the dissociative experiences scale against the criterion of the SCID-D, using receiver operating characteristics (ROC) analysis. *Dissociation, 6*(4): 28–38.

Ellason, J. W., Ross, C. A., Mayran, L. W. & Sainton, K. (1991). Convergent validity of the new form of the DES. *Dissociation, 11*(2): 101–103.

Figley, C. R. (1986). Compassion fatigue as secondary traumatic stress disorder: An overview. In C. R. Figley (Ed.), *Compassion Fatigue: Coping with secondary traumatic stress disorder in those who treat the traumatized.* New York: Brunner/Mazel.

Fine, C. G. (1991). Treatment stabilisation and crisis prevention: Pacing the therapy of the multiple personality disorder patient. *Psychiatric Clinics of North America, 14*(3): 661–676.

Holloway, E. A. (2007). Integrated breathing and relaxation training (the Papworth method) for adults with asthma in primary care: A randomised controlled trial. *Thorax, 62*(12): 1,039–1,042.

International Society for the Study of Dissociation (2004). Guidelines for the evaluation and treatment of dissociative symptoms in children and adolescents. *Journal of Trauma and Dissociation, 5*(3): 119–150. (Updated April 2010) Available at: *www.isst-d.org/education/childguidelines-ISSTD-2003.pdf* [Accessed 28 March 2012].

International Statistical Classification of Diseases & Related Health Problems. Tenth Version. World Health Organization (2007). Geneva: World Health Organization.

Janet, P. (1935). Realisation and interpretation. In: Van der Hart, O., Steele, K., Boon, S. & Brown, P. (1993). The treatment of traumatic memories: Synthesis realisation and integration. *Dissociation, 6*: 162–180.

Kennerley, H. (1997). *Overcoming Anxiety.* London: Robinson.

Kluft, R. P. (1984). An introduction to multiple personality disorder. *Psychiatric Annals*, *14*: 19–24.

Kluft, R. P. (1991). Clinical presentations of multiple personality disorder. *Psychiatric Clinics of North America*, *14*(3): 605–629.

Kluft, R. P. & Fine, C. G (Eds.) (1993). *Clinical Perspectives on Multiple Personality Disorder*. Washington, DC: American Psychiatric Press Inc.

Lamagna, J. & Gleiser, K. A. (2007). Building a secure internal attachment: An intra-relational approach to ego strengthening and emotional processing with chronically traumatised clients. *Journal of Trauma & Dissociation*, *8*(1): 25–52.

Lemke, W. (2007). Fostering internal communication through the use of imagery in the treatment of dissociative identity disorder. *Journal of Trauma & Dissociation*, *8*(4): 53–68.

Loewenstein, R. J. (1991). An office mental state examination for complex chronic dissociative symptoms and multiple personality disorder. *Psychiatric Clinics of North America*, *14*(3): 567–603.

Mazur, M. Dissociative Identity Disorder and the cycle of violence. (Updated May 2011) Available at: *www.globalpolitician.com/print.asp?id=6054* [Accessed 28 March 2012].

Moskowitz, A. (2004). Dissociation and violence: A review of the literature. *Trauma, Violence, Abuse*, *(1)*: 21–46.

Nijenhuis, E. R. S. (2003). The scoring and interpretation of the SDQ 20 and the SDQ5 update. (Updated 29 April 2010) Available at: www.enijenhuis. nl/SDQ/sdq-update.doc [Accessed 28 March 2012].

Nijenhuis, E. R. S., Spinhoven, P., Van Dyck, R., Van der Hart, O. & Vanderlinden, J. (1996). The development and psychometric characteristics of the somatoform dissociation questionnaire (SDQ-20). *The Journal of Nervous & Mental Disease*, *184*(1): 688–694.

Nijenhuis, E. R. S., Spinhoven, P., Van Dyck, R., Van der Hart, O. & Vanderlinden, J. (1997). The development of the somatoform questionnaire (SDQ-5) as a screening instrument for dissociative disorders. *Acta Psychiatrica Scandinavica*, *96*: 311–318.

Owen, W. (2005). Relaxation Emporium. Available at: *www.relaxationemporium.com/relaxationtechniquespart2.html* [Accessed 28 March 2012].

Pearlman L. A. & Saakvitne K. W. (1995). *Trauma and the Therapist: Countertransference and vicarious traumatisation in psychotherapy with incest survivors*. New York: W.W. Norton.

Putnam, F. W. (1989). *Diagnosis and Treatment of Multiple Personality Disorder*. London: The Guilford Press.

Ringrose, J. L. (2010). "Working psychotherapeutically with the dissociative disorders—an exploration of contemporary theory and practice" (unpublished doctoral thesis, Metanoia Institute, 2010).

Ringrose, J. L. (2011). Meeting the needs of clients with dissociative identity disorder: Considerations for psychotherapy. *British Journal of Guidance & Counselling*, *38*(4): 1–13.

Ross, C. A. (1997). *Dissociative Identity Disorder: Diagnosis, clinical features and treatment of multiple personality disorder*. New York: Wiley.

Ross C. A., Norton, G. R. & Wozney, K. (1989). Multiple personality disorder: An analysis of 236 cases. *Canadian Journal of Psychiatry*, *34*: 413–417.

Ross, C. A., Heber, S., Norton, G. R. & Anderson, G. (1989a). Somatic symptoms in multiple personality disorder. *Psychosomatics*, *30*(2): 154–160.

Ross, C. A., Heber, S., Norton, G. R., Anderson, D., Anderson, G. & Bruchet, P. (1989b). The dissociative disorders interview schedule: A structured interview. *Dissociation*, *11*(3): 169–189.

Ross, C. A., Anderson, G., Fleisher, W. P. & Norton, G. R. (1991). The frequency of multiple personality disorder among psychiatric patients. *American Journal of Society*, *148*: 1,717–1,720.

Simeon, D. & Abugel, J. (2006). *Feeling Unreal*. Oxford: Oxford University Press.

Simeon, D., Guralnik, O., Gross, S., Stein, D. J., Schmeidler, J. & Hollander, E. (1998). The detection and measurement of depersonalisation disorder. *The Journal of Nervous and Mental Disease*, *186*(9): 536–542.

Sirius (2011). Alternatives to self-harm. Available at: *www.siriusproject.org/alternatives.htm* [Accessed 28 March 2012].

Steinberg, M. (1994). *Structured Clinical Interview for DSM-IV Dissociative Disorders—Revised (SCID-D-R)*. Washington, DC: American Psychiatric Press.

Steinberg, M. & Schnall, M. (2000). *The Stranger in the Mirror: Dissociation the Hidden Epidemic*. New York: Quill Publications.

Steinberg, M., Cichetti, D. V., Buchanan, J., Hall, P. & Rounsaville, B. (1993). Clinical assessment of dissociative symptoms and disorders: The structured clinical interview for DSM-IV dissociative disorders. *Dissociation*, *6*: 3–16.

Tatarelli, R., Pompili, M. & Girardi, P. (2007). *Suicide in Psychiatric Disorders*. New York: Nova Science Publishers.

Thomas, P. M. (2005). Dissociation and internal models of protection: Psychotherapy and child abuse survivors. *Psychotherapy, Research, Practice & Training*, *42*(1): 20–36.

Turkus, J. A. (1991). Psychotherapy and case management for multiple personality disorder: Synthesis for continuity of care. *Psychiatric Clinics of North America*, *14*(3): 649–660.

Van der Hart, O., Nijenhuis, E. R. S. & Steel, K. (2006). *The Haunted Self: Structural Dissociation and the Treatment of Chronic Traumatisation.* New York: W.W. Norton & Co.

Van der Hart, O., Steel, K., Boon, S. & Brown, P. (1993). The treatment of traumatic memories: Synthesis, realisation and integration. *Dissociation*, 6: 162–180.

Warner, M. S. (1998). A client-centred approach to therapeutic work with dissociated and fragile process. In: L. S. Greenberg, J. C. Watson & G. Lietaer (Eds.), *Handbook of Experiential Psychotherapy (pp. 368–387).* New York: Guilford Press.

INDEX

Abugel, J. 88
accident and emergency (A&E)
    departments 12, 30, 90
agitation 116
alter personalities 4, 6–7, 57, 61, 93,
    112
American Psychiatric Association
    3–4
amnesia 3, 13, 16, 20, 58
anger 33–34, 55, 87, 116
anxiety 12–13, 23, 31–33, 55, 63,
    71–72, 76–77, 81, 88, 107–108,
    111
    managing 7, 33, 107
    provoking situations 79
anxiety-provoking 72, 77, 81
    rehearsing 79
apparently normal personality
    (ANP) 6
Aquarone, Remy, 15

assessment and diagnosis 11, 20–22
    assessment of the client's
        functioning 15
    stronger emphasis on 11
auditory hallucinations 13

behavioural distractions 73–74, 81
behaviours, affect, sensations,
    and knowledge (BASK) 61
    components 50, 53
    elements 61
    model 49–50, 53, 56
Bernstein, D. A. 71, 107
bipolar disorder see schizoid
    tendency
black and white thinking and
    exaggeration 78, 81
borderline personality disorder
    12
Borkovec, T. D. 71, 107

...tion can be obtained
...ng.com
...USA
...501300122
...LV00014B/461